Cambridge Latin Course

soothsayer
says
sooths

Name Stella Pandian -
Molenscra

Form LVMD

Cambridge Latin Course

Book III
FOURTH EDITION

CAMBRIDGE
UNIVERSITY PRESS

CAMBRIDGE
UNIVERSITY PRESS

University Printing House, Cambridge CB2 8BS, United Kingdom

One Liberty Plaza, 20th Floor, New York, NY 10006, USA

477 Williamstown Road, Port Melbourne, VIC 3207, Australia

4843/24, 2nd Floor, Ansari Road, Daryaganj, Delhi – 110002, India

79 Anson Road, #06–04/06, Singapore 079906

Cambridge University Press is part of the University of Cambridge.

It furthers the University's mission by disseminating knowledge in the pursuit of education, learning and research at the highest international levels of excellence.

Information on this title: education.cambridge.org

This book, an outcome of work jointly commissioned by the Schools Council before its closure and the Cambridge School Classics Project, is published under the aegis of Qualifications and Curriculum Authority Enterprises Limited, 83 Piccadilly, London W1J 8QA.

First published 1972
7th printing 1982
Second edition 1983
9th printing 1989
Integrated edition 1990
10th printing 1999
Fourth edition 2001
40 39 38 37 36 35 34 33 32 31 30 29 28 27 26 25 24 23 22 21 20

Printed in Poland by Opolgraf

A catalogue record for this publication is available from the British Library

ISBN 978-0-521-79794-8 Paperback

Cambridge University Press has no responsibility for the persistence or accuracy of URLs for external or third-party internet websites referred to in this publication, and does not guarantee that any content on such websites is, or will remain, accurate or appropriate.

Cover photographs: front, Roger Dalladay; back, Kunsthistorisches Museum, Vienna
Map by Reg Piggott
Drawings by Peter Kesteven, Joy Mellor and Leslie Jones

....

ACKNOWLEDGEMENTS

Thanks are due to the following for permission to reproduce photographs and drawings: p. 1, p. 25, p. 28 r, p. 50 b, p. 51 r, p. 100, p. 143, © Copyright The British Museum; p. 17 r, p. 19 b, p. 21, p. 34, HAB White; p. 18 t, p. 138 b, Society of Antiquaries of London; p. 19 t, Bath Archaeological Trust; p. 20, p. 52 l, Roman Baths Museum, Bath; p. 36, Institute of Archaeology, Oxford; p. 37, © Photo RMN – H. Lewandowski; p. 49 l, p. 69 b, Scala; p. 54, Cambridge University Museum of Archaeology and Anthropology; p. 55, Musée du Bardo; p. 62, Cambridge University Committee for Aerial Photography; p. 69 t, CSCP; p. 101 b, p. 103, Trustees of the National Museums of Scotland; p. 104, Colchester Castle Museum; p. 116, p. 118 t, Grosvenor Museum, Chester; p. 121, Kunsthistorisches Museum, Vienna; p. 135 b, Penguin Books/Scala; p. 136, English Heritage; p. 137, Northamptonshire Archaeology; p. 138, Whitby Museum.

Other photography by Roger Dalladay. Thanks are due to the following for permission to reproduce photographs: p. 85, p. 86, The Ermine Street Guard.

Every effort has been made to reach copyright holders. The publishers would be glad to hear from anyone whose rights they have unknowingly infringed.

Contents

Stage 21   Aquae Sūlis   page 1

Stage 22   dēfīxiō   21

Stage 23   haruspex   37

Stage 24   fuga   55

Stage 25   mīlitēs   71

Stage 26   Agricola   89

Stage 27   in castrīs   105

Stage 28   imperium   121

Language information   143

     Part One: About the language   146

     Part Two: Vocabulary   168

AQUAE SULIS

STAGE 21

1   in oppidō Aquīs Sūlis labōrābant multī fabrī, quī thermās
maximās exstruēbant. architectus Rōmānus fabrōs
īnspiciēbat.

2   faber prīmus statuam deae Sūlis faciēbat.
architectus fabrum laudāvit, quod perītus erat et dīligenter
labōrābat.
faber, ab architectō laudātus, laetissimus erat.

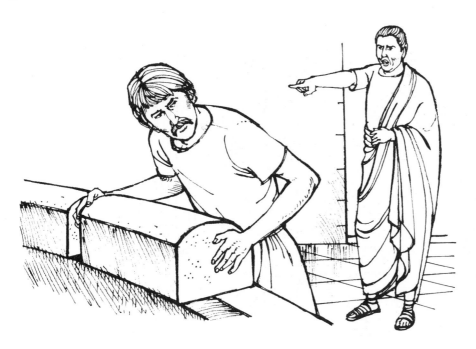

3 faber secundus mūrum circum fontem pōnēbat.
   architectus fabrum incitāvit, quod fessus erat et lentē
   labōrābat.
   faber, ab architectō incitātus, rem graviter ferēbat. nihil tamen
   dīxit, quod architectum timēbat.

4 faber tertius aquam ad balneum ē fonte sacrō portābat.
   architectus fabrum vituperāvit, quod ignāvus erat et minimē
   labōrābat.
   faber, ab architectō vituperātus, īnsolenter respondit.

5 architectus, ubi verba īnsolentia fabrī audīvit, servōs suōs
   arcessīvit.
   servī, ab architectō arcessītī, fabrum comprehendērunt et in
   balneum dēiēcērunt.

6 'linguam sordidam habēs', inquit architectus cachinnāns.
   'melius est tibi aquam sacram bibere.'

fōns sacer

fōns *fountain, spring*

Quīntus apud Salvium manēbat per tōtam hiemem. saepe ad
aulam Cogidubnī ībat, ā rēge invītātus. Quīntus eī multa dē urbe
Alexandrīā nārrābat, quod rēx aliquid novī audīre semper
volēbat.

    ubi vēr appropinquābat, Cogidubnus in morbum gravem
incidit. multī medicī, ad aulam arcessītī, remedium morbī
quaesīvērunt. ingravēscēbat tamen morbus. rēx Quīntum et
Salvium dē remediō anxius cōnsuluit.

    'mī Quīnte', inquit, 'tū es vir sapiēns. volō tē mihi cōnsilium
dare. ad fontem sacrum īre dēbeō?'

    'ubi est iste fōns?' rogāvit Quīntus.

    'est in oppidō Aquīs Sūlis', inquit Cogidubnus. 'multī aegrōtī,
quī ex illō fonte aquam bibērunt, posteā convaluērunt.
architectus Rōmānus, ā mē missus, thermās maximās ibi
exstrūxit. prope thermās stat templum deae Sūlis, ā meīs fabrīs
aedificātum. ego deam saepe honōrāvī; nunc fortasse dea mē
sānāre potest. Salvī, tū es vir magnae calliditātis; volō tē mihi
cōnsilium dare. quid facere dēbeō?'

    'tū es vir magnae sapientiae', respondit ille. 'melius est tibi
testāmentum facere.'

5

morbum: morbus *illness*
gravem: gravis *serious*
cōnsuluit: cōnsulere *consult*
cōnsilium *advice*
oppidō: oppidum *town*
Aquīs Sūlis: Aquae Sūlis
   Bath

10

aegrōtī: aegrōtus *invalid*
convaluērunt: convalēscere
   get better, recover
exstrūxit: exstruere *build*
vir magnae calliditātis *a man*
   of great shrewdness,
   cleverness

15

sapientiae: sapientia *wisdom*
testāmentum *will*

20

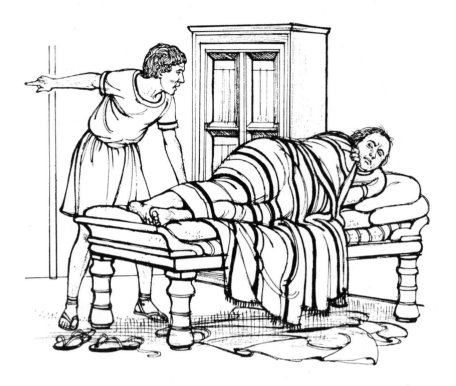

Lūcius Marcius Memor

When you have read this story, answer the questions at the end.

oppidum Aquae Sūlis parvum erat, thermae maximae.
prōcūrātor thermārum erat Lūcius Marcius Memor, nōtissimus
haruspex, homō obēsus et ignāvus. quamquam iam tertia hōra
erat, Memor in cubiculō ēbrius dormiēbat. Cephalus, haruspicis
lībertus, Memorem excitāre temptābat.   5
    'domine! domine!' clāmābat.
    haruspex, graviter dormiēns, nihil respondit.
    'dominus nimium vīnī rūrsus bibit', sibi dīxit lībertus.
'domine! surge! hōra tertia est.'
    Memor, ā lībertō tandem excitātus, ūnum oculum aperuit.   10
    'fer mihi plūs vīnī!' inquit. 'tum abī!'
    'domine! domine! necesse est tibi surgere', inquit Cephalus.
    'cūr mē vexās, Cephale?' inquit Memor. 'cūr tū rem
administrāre ipse nōn potes?'
    'rem huius modī administrāre nōn possum', respondit   15
lībertus. 'sunt multī servī, multī fabrī, quī mandāta prōcūrātōris
exspectant. tē exspectat architectus ipse, vir magnae dignitātis.
tē exspectant aegrōtī. adsunt mīlitēs, ab hostibus vulnerātī.
adsunt nōnnūllī mercātōrēs, quōs arcessīvistī. tū rem ipse
administrāre dēbēs.'   20

prōcūrātor manager
haruspex soothsayer
obēsus fat

graviter heavily, soundly
nimium vīnī too much wine
rūrsus again

fer! bring!
plūs vīnī more wine

huius modī of this kind
mandāta instructions, orders
dignitātis: dignitās
   importance, prestige
hostibus: hostis enemy

'numquam dēsinit labor', clāmāvit Memor. 'quam fessus sum! cūr ad hunc populum barbarum umquam vēnī? vīta mea est dūra. nam in Britanniā ad magnōs honōrēs ascendere nōn possum. necesse est mihi virōs potentēs colere. ēheu! in hāc īnsulā sunt paucī virī potentēs, paucī clārī.'   25

'quid vīs mē facere, Memor?' inquit lībertus.

'iubeō tē omnēs dīmittere', clāmāvit Memor. 'nōlī mē iterum vexāre!'

Memor, postquam haec verba dīxit, statim obdormīvit. Cephalus, ā dominō īrātō territus, invītus exiit. in thermīs   30 plūrimōs hominēs invēnit, vehementer clāmantēs et Memorem absentem vituperantēs. eōs omnēs Cephalus dīmīsit.

dēsinit: dēsinere *end, cease*
labor *work*
populum: populus *people*
umquam *ever*
honōrēs: honor *honour, public position*
potentēs: potēns *powerful*
colere *cultivate, make friends with*
paucī *few*
clārī: clārus *famous, distinguished*
haec verba *these words*
territus: terrēre *frighten*
absentem: absēns *absent*

Questions

		Marks
1	**oppidum … maximae.** Why might a visitor to Aquae Sulis have been surprised on seeing the town and its baths?	1
2	**prōcūrātor … ignāvus** (lines 2–3). Read this sentence and look at the picture. Which two Latin adjectives describe Memor as he appears in the picture? Translate them.	2
3	**tertia hōra** (line 3). Was this early or late in the morning? Give a reason for your answer.	1
4	In line 7, the soothsayer is described as **graviter dormiēns**. Which Latin word in line 4 explains the reason for this? What does this word and the word **rūrsus** (line 8) suggest about Memor?	2
5	After Memor was awake, what two orders did he give to Cephalus? What did he think Cephalus could do (lines 11–14)?	2 + 1
6	**mandāta prōcūrātōris** (line 16). Why do you think Cephalus used these words rather than **mandāta tua**?	1
7	**numquam … fessus sum** (lines 21–2). What do you think Cephalus' reaction would be on hearing Memor say this? Give a reason for your answer.	2
8	**ad magnōs honōrēs ascendere nōn possum** (lines 23–4). What, according to Memor, is the reason for his failure?	2
9	In lines 27–9 how did Memor react to Cephalus' question? Make three points.	3
10	Which two Latin words show how Cephalus was feeling when he left Memor's bedroom?	2
11	What did he find when he arrived in the baths (lines 30–2)?	2
12	Read Cephalus' speech in lines 15–20 again. Pick out two different words or phrases which he repeats and suggest why he used each of them to try to get Memor to act.	2 + 2

TOTAL **25**

senātor advenit

Cephalus ā thermīs rediit. cubiculum rūrsus intrāvit
Memoremque dormientem excitāvit. Memor, simulac
Cephalum vīdit, īrātus clāmāvit,
    'cūr prohibēs mē dormīre? cūr mihi nōn pārēs? stultior es
quam asinus.'   5
    'sed domine', inquit Cephalus, 'aliquid novī nūntiāre volō.
postquam hinc discessī, mandāta, quae mihi dedistī, effēcī. ubi
tamen aegrōtōs fabrōsque dīmittēbam, senātōrem thermīs
appropinquantem cōnspexī.'
    Memor, valdē vexātus,   10
    'quis est ille senātor?' inquit. 'unde vēnit? senātōrem vidēre
nōlō.'
    'melius est tibi hunc senātōrem vidēre', inquit Cephalus.
'nam Gāius Salvius est.'
    'num Gāius Salvius Līberālis?' exclāmāvit Memor. 'nōn   15
crēdō tibi.'
    Cephalus tamen facile eī persuāsit, quod Salvius iam in
āream thermārum equitābat.
    Memor perterritus statim clāmāvit,
    'fer mihi togam! fer calceōs! ōrnāmenta mea ubi sunt? vocā   20
servōs! quam īnfēlīx sum! Salvius hūc venit, vir summae
auctōritātis, quem colere maximē volō.'
    Memor celerrimē togam calceōsque induit. Cephalus eī
ōrnāmenta trādidit, ex armāriō raptim extracta. haruspex
lībertum innocentem vituperābat, lībertus Salvium.   25

prohibēs: prohibēre *prevent*
pārēs: pārēre *obey*
hinc *from here*
effēcī: efficere *carry out,*
    accomplish

calceōs: calceus *shoe*
ōrnāmenta *decorations*
auctōritātis: auctōritās
    authority
raptim *hastily, quickly*

*Memor set up a statue near the
altar of the goddess Sulis. The
statue has disappeared, but this is
the statue base with his name on it.
The altar is in the background.*

About the language: perfect passive participles

1   In Stage 20, you met sentences like these, containing present participles:

> servī per vīllam contendērunt, dominum **quaerentēs**.
> *The slaves hurried through the house, **looking for** their master.*

> puella mātrem in hortō **sedentem** vīdit.
> *The girl saw her mother **sitting** in the garden.*

2   In Stage 21, you have met sentences like these:

> Memor, ā lībertō **excitātus**, īrātissimus erat.
> *Memor, **having been awakened** by the freedman, was very angry.*

> thermae, ā Rōmānīs **aedificātae**, maximae erant.
> *The baths, **having been built** by the Romans, were very big.*

The words in **bold type** are perfect passive participles.

3   A participle is used to describe a noun. For instance, in the first example in paragraph 2, **excitātus** describes Memor. Participles change their endings to agree with the nouns they describe. In this way they behave like adjectives. Compare the following pair of sentences:

> *singular*   faber, ab architectō **laudātus**, rīsit.
> *The craftsman, **having been praised** by the architect, smiled.*

> *plural*   fabrī, ab architectō **laudātī**, rīsērunt.
> *The craftsmen, **having been praised** by the architect, smiled.*

4   Translate the following examples:

a   servus, ā dominō verberātus, ex oppidō fūgit.
b   nūntiī, ā rēge arcessītī, rem terribilem nārrāvērunt.
c   ancilla, ā Quīntō laudāta, laetissima erat.
d   templum, ā fabrīs perītīs aedificātum, erat splendidum.
e   mīlitēs, ab hostibus vulnerātī, thermās vīsitāre voluērunt.
f   uxor, ā marītō vexāta, ē vīllā discessit.

In each sentence, write down the perfect passive participle and the noun which it describes. State whether each pair is singular or plural.

5 Notice that the perfect passive participle can be translated in a number of ways:

> architectus, ā Cogidubnō ipsō missus, thermās exstrūxit.
> *The architect, having been sent by Cogidubnus himself, built the baths.*

Or, in more natural English:
> *The architect, sent by Cogidubnus himself, built the baths.*

> servī, ā dominō arcessītī, statim ad tablīnum festīnāvērunt.
> *The slaves, having been summoned by their master, hurried at once to the study.*

Or, in more natural English:
> *When the slaves had been summoned by their master, they hurried at once to the study.*

Memor rem suscipit

I

Salvius et Memor, in hortō sōlī ambulantēs, sermōnem gravem habent.

Salvius:	Lūcī Marcī Memor, vir summae prūdentiae es. volō tē rem magnam suscipere.	**prūdentiae: prūdentia** *good sense, intelligence*
Memor:	tālem rem suscipere velim, sed occupātissimus sum. 5 exspectant mē aegrōtī et sacerdōtēs. vexant mē architectus et fabrī. sed quid vīs mē facere?	**tālem: tālis** *such* **velim** *I should like*
Salvius:	Tiberius Claudius Cogidubnus, rēx Rēgnēnsium, hūc nūper advēnit. Cogidubnus, quī in morbum gravem incidit, aquam ē fonte sacrō bibere vult. 10	
Memor:	difficile est mihi tē adiuvāre, mī senātor. Cogidubnus est vir octōgintā annōrum. difficile est deae Sūlī Cogidubnum sānāre.	**octōgintā** *eighty* **annōrum: annus** *year*
Salvius:	nōlō tē reddere Cogidubnum sānum. volō tē rem contrāriam efficere. 15	**reddere** *make* **sānum: sānus** *well, healthy* **rem contrāriam: rēs contrāria** *the opposite*
Memor:	quid dīcis? num mortem Cogidubnī cupis?	
Salvius:	ita vērō! porrō, quamquam tam occupātus es, volō tē ipsum hanc rem efficere.	**porrō** *what's more, furthermore*
Memor:	vīsne mē rēgem interficere? rem huius modī facere nōlō. Cogidubnus enim est vir clārissimus, ā populō 20 Rōmānō honōrātus.	

Salvius: es vir summae calliditātis. hanc rem efficere potes. nōn sōlum ego, sed etiam Imperātor, hoc cupit. Cogidubnus enim Rōmānōs saepe vexāvit. Imperātor mihi, nōn Cogidubnō, cōnfīdit. Imperātor tibi praemium dignum prōmittit. num praemium, ab Imperātōre prōmissum, recūsāre vīs?

Memor: quō modō rem facere possum?

Salvius: nescio. hoc tantum tibi dīcō: Imperātor mortem Cogidubnī exspectat.

Memor: ō mē miserum! rem difficiliōrem numquam fēcī.

Salvius: vīta, mī Memor, est plēna rērum difficilium. (*exit Salvius.*)

nōn sōlum ... sed etiam *not only ... but also*
dignum: dignus *worthy, appropriate*
recūsāre *refuse*
nescio: nescīre *not know*

II

Memor: Cephale! Cephale! (*lībertus, ā Memore vocātus, celeriter intrat. pōculum vīnī fert.*) cūr mihi vīnum offers? nōn vīnum, sed cōnsilium quaerō. iubeō tē mihi cōnsilium quam celerrimē dare. rēx Cogidubnus hūc vēnit, remedium morbī petēns. Imperātor, ā Cogidubnō saepe vexātus, iam mortem eius cupit. Imperātor ipse iubet mē hoc efficere. quam difficile est!

Cephalus: minimē, facile est! pōculum venēnātum habeō, mihi ā latrōne Aegyptiō ōlim datum. venēnum, in pōculō cēlātum, vītam celerrimē exstinguere potest.

Memor: cōnsilium, quod mihi prōpōnis, perīculōsum est. Cogidubnō venēnum dare timeō.

Cephalus: nihil perīculī est. rēx, quotiēns ē balneō exiit, ad fontem deae īre solet. tum necesse est servō prope fontem deae stāre et pōculum rēgī praebēre.

Memor: (*dēlectātus*) cōnsilium optimum est. nūllīs tamen servīs cōnfīdō. sed tibi cōnfīdō, Cephale. iubeō tē ipsum Cogidubnō pōculum praebēre.

Cephalus: ēheu! mihi rem difficillimam impōnis.

Memor: vīta, mī Cephale, est plēna rērum difficilium.

venēnātum: venēnātus *poisoned*
datum: dare *give*
venēnum *poison*
exstinguere *extinguish, destroy*
prōpōnis: prōpōnere *propose, put forward*
nihil perīculī *no danger*
quotiēns *whenever*
balneō: balneum *bath*
praebēre *offer, provide*
difficillimam: difficillimus *very difficult*
impōnis: impōnere *impose*

Word patterns: adjectives and adverbs

1   Study the form and meaning of the following words:

laet**us**	*happy*	laet**ē**	*happily*
perīt**us**	*skilled*	perīt**ē**	*skilfully*
stultissim**us**	*very foolish*	stultissim**ē**	*very foolishly*

2   As you already know, the words in the left-hand columns are adjectives. The words on the right are known as adverbs

3   Using the pattern in paragraph 1 as a guide, complete the following table:

adjectives		*adverbs*	
cautus	*cautious*	cautē	. . . .
superbus	*proud*	. . . .	*proudly*
crūdēlissimus	*very cruel*	. . . .	. . . .

4   Divide the following words into two lists, one of adjectives and one of adverbs. Then give the meaning of each word.

   intentē, gravissimus, callidus, tacitē, ignāvus, dīligentissimus, firmē, saevissimē.

5   Choose the correct Latin words to translate the words in **bold type** in the following sentences:

   a   Memor was a **very hard** master. (dūrissimus, dūrissimē)
   b   The merchant always treated his customers **honestly**. (probus, probē)
   c   The senator **very generously** promised a large donation. (līberālissimus, līberālissimē)
   d   A **cautious** (cautus, cautē) man proceeds **slowly**. (lentus, lentē)

Practising the language

1 Complete each sentence with the right case of the noun. Then translate the sentence.

   a omnēs aegrōtī . . . . vīsitāre volēbant. (fōns, fontem, fontis)
   b plūrimī servī in fundō . . . . labōrābant. (dominus, dominum, dominī)
   c 'fortasse . . . . morbum meum sānāre potest', inquit rēx. (dea, deam, deae)
   d . . . . Cogidubnum laudāvērunt, quod līberālis et sapiēns erat. (prīncipēs, prīncipum)
   e mercātor, postquam . . . . accēpit, ē forō discessit. (dēnāriī, dēnāriōs, dēnāriōrum)
   f senex, quī in Aegyptō diū habitāverat, magnum numerum . . . . comparāverat. (statuae, statuās, statuārum)

2 Translate each English sentence into Latin by selecting correctly from the pairs of Latin words.

   For example: *The messenger heard the voice of the old man.*
      nūntius   vōcem   senem   audīvī
      nūntium   vōcī   senis   audīvit
   Latin translation: nūntius vōcem senis audīvit.

   a *The priests showed the statue to the architect.*
      sacerdōtēs   statuam   architectum   ostendit
      sacerdōtibus   statuās   architectō   ostendērunt
   b *The king praised the skilful doctor.*
      rēx   medicus   perītum   laudāvit
      rēgēs   medicum   perītī   laudāvērunt
   c *A friend of the soldiers was visiting the temple.*
      amīcus   mīlitis   templum   vīsitābat
      amīcō   mīlitum   templī   vīsitāvit
   d *The shouts of the invalids had annoyed the soothsayer.*
      clāmōrem   aegrōtī   haruspicem   vexāverant
      clāmōrēs   aegrōtōrum   haruspicēs   vexāvērunt
   e *We handed over the master's money to the farmers.*
      pecūnia   dominum   agricolās   trādidimus
      pecūniam   dominī   agricolīs   trādidērunt

3 Complete each sentence with the right word. Then translate the sentence.

   a tū ipse hanc rem administrāre . . . . (dēbeō, dēbēs, dēbet)
   b cūr mē vituperās? herī per tōtum diem . . . . (labōrāvī, labōrāvistī, labōrāvit)
   c ego, quod fontem sacrum vidēre . . . ., iter ad oppidum Aquās Sūlis fēcī. (cupiēbam, cupiēbās, cupiēbat)
   d lībertus, quī senātōrem . . . ., in cubiculum haruspicis ruit. (cōnspexeram, cōnspexerās, cōnspexerat)
   e ē lectō surrēxī, quod dormīre nōn . . . . (poteram, poterās, poterat)
   f in hāc vīllā . . . . Memor, haruspex nōtissimus. (habitō, habitās, habitat)

Aquae Sulis and its baths

The Roman town of Aquae Sulis lies beneath the modern city of Bath in the valley of the river Avon. In a small area of low-lying ground, enclosed by a bend in the river, mineral springs of hot water emerge from underground at the rate of over a million litres a day and at a temperature of between 46 and 49 degrees centigrade. The water we see today fell as rain 10,000 years ago and then percolated two miles down into the earth before rising to the surface as hot springs. These have a low mineral content, consisting mainly of calcium, magnesium and sodium.

Long before the Romans came, the springs were regarded as a sacred place. The Celts who lived on the surrounding hills came to worship their goddess Sulis there and believed in her power to cure their illnesses through immersion in the hot spring waters.

When the Romans arrived they were quick to recognise the importance and potential of the springs as a place of pilgrimage. They erected a set of huge public baths so that visitors could enjoy their experience of the hot springs in comfort.

The most important part of the baths complex was the sacred spring. The Romans enclosed it in a large reservoir lined with lead and surrounded by a simple stone balustrade. The pool with its bubbling waters overhung with clouds of steam presented an awesome and mysterious sight to the many visitors to the baths.

The main building was a long, rectangular structure, possibly the largest and most magnificent set of baths west of Rome at this date. It contained three main plunge baths filled with a constant supply of water at a pleasant temperature. The water was brought from the spring through lead pipes. The pool nearest the spring naturally contained the hottest water, whereas the furthest pool was the coolest, since the water lost much of its heat on the way to it. There was also a suite of warm and hot baths heated by a hypocaust.

Some people travelled long distances to Aquae Sulis, attracted by the fame of its spring and its healing powers. No doubt the heat of the water relieved conditions such as rheumatism and arthritis, but many people must have visited the spring in the hope of miraculous cures for all kinds of diseases. One elderly woman, Rusonia Aventina, came from Metz in eastern Gaul. Her tombstone shows that she died at Aquae Sulis at the age of fifty-eight, perhaps from the illness which she had hoped the spring would cure. Julius Vitalis was a soldier serving as armourer to the Twentieth Legion, based at Chester. His tombstone records that he had served for just nine

The largest of the three plunge baths at Bath: it is now called the Great Bath. Notice the steam rising from the naturally hot water.

years when he died at the age of twenty-nine; possibly his commanding officer had sent him to Aquae Sulis on sick leave.

Many visitors seeing the mysterious steaming waters would feel that they were in a holy place. They would believe that a cure for their ailments depended as much on divine favour as on the medicinal powers of the water. A temple was therefore constructed next to the bath buildings and the enclosed area round the temple, the sacred precinct, included the spring within its boundaries. A magnificent altar stood in front of the

Above: How the Great Bath probably looked around the time of our story, late first century AD.
Below: A portrait of a lady with fashionable hairstyle. From her tomb at Bath.

temple and a life-size gilt bronze statue of the goddess Sulis Minerva was inside, glowing with golden hues in the flickering light of the eternal flame. By linking the name Minerva to that of Sulis in this way, the Romans encouraged the Britons to recognise the power of the Roman goddess of healing, wisdom and the arts and associate it with that of the Sulis they already knew.

When the temple precinct was excavated the stone base of a statue was found. The inscription on the base records that the statue was dedicated to the goddess Sulis by a Roman official, Lucius Marcius Memor (see the photograph on page 8). Nothing more is known about him but his presence in Bath may be another example of the Romans' efforts to spread Roman ways and customs among the Britons. Many such officials must have contributed to the policy of romanisation in this way.

The baths and temple about AD100

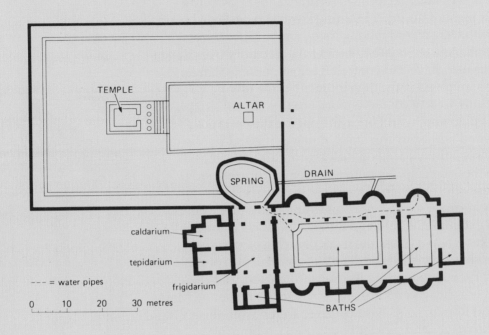

TEMPLE

ALTAR

SPRING

DRAIN

caldarium

tepidarium

frigidarium

- - - = water pipes

0   10   20   30 metres

BATHS

Water ran from the spring to the baths through lead pipes.

In addition to the pools of natural hot water, there was a set of baths heated by a hypocaust in the Roman manner, with a caldarium, tepidarium and frigidarium. Part of the hypocaust is seen below.

At the time of our story (AD 83), Aquae Sulis was a small but growing community. The complex of bath buildings and temple was the most impressive feature of the town. There were probably a few other public buildings, such as a basilica for the administration of law and local government, and possibly a theatre, but most of the other buildings would have been houses for those who were already living there, and inns for the town's many visitors. Aquae Sulis lay within tribal territory over which Cogidubnus may have had control. It is just possible that he himself was involved in the development of the town.

Aquae Sulis was, of course, a tourist centre as well as a place of religious pilgrimage, and one can imagine the entrance to the baths crowded with souvenir stalls, much as it is today. Visitors would buy such things as good luck charms and offerings to throw into the sacred spring with a prayer for future good health. These offerings were sometimes expensive: they included beautifully carved gemstones and items of jewellery.

The full extent of the bath and temple buildings is gradually becoming known to us from the work of archaeologists. Excavations have revealed the details of construction of the Roman reservoir surrounding the hot spring itself, and the results of these excavations are on display in the museum. Many thousands of Roman coins have been recovered from the spring, together with silver and pewter bowls used for pouring offerings to the goddess. About ninety small sheets of lead or pewter were also found with Latin inscriptions on them. Their translations show that some people were anxious to use the powers of Sulis Minerva for unpleasant purposes, as will be seen in the next Stage.

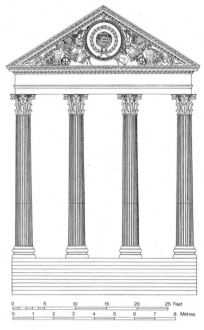

Above: *Reconstruction of the temple front.*
Left: *A model of the temple in its courtyard.*

Some of the objects people threw into the spring.

Vocabulary checklist 21

From now on, most verbs in the checklists are listed as in the Book III Language Information section (i.e. perfect passive participles are usually included).

ā, ab	*from; by*
adiuvō, adiuvāre, adiūvī	*help*
annus, annī	*year*
cēlō, cēlāre, cēlāvī, cēlātus	*hide*
circum	*around*
dūrus, dūra, dūrum	*harsh, hard*
efficiō, efficere, effēcī, effectus	*carry out, accomplish*
fōns, fontis	*fountain, spring*
gravis, grave	*heavy, serious*
hōra, hōrae	*hour*
īnfēlīx, *gen.* īnfēlīcis	*unlucky*
iubeō, iubēre, iussī, iussus	*order*
morbus, morbī	*illness*
nōnnūllī, nōnnūllae	*some, several*
nūper	*recently*
oppidum, oppidī	*town*
plēnus, plēna, plēnum	*full*
plūs, *gen.* plūris	*more*
pretium, pretiī	*price*
sacer, sacra, sacrum	*sacred*
sapiēns, *gen.* sapientis	*wise*
unde	*from where*

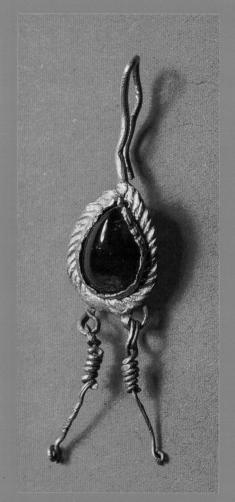

A carbuncle earring found in the spring.

DEFIXIO

STAGE 22

1 fūr thermās cautē intrāvit.
fūr, thermās ingressus, ad fontem
sacrum festīnāvit.

2 fūr, prope fontem stāns,
circumspectāvit.
fūr, senem cōnspicātus, post
columnam sē cēlāvit.

3 senex, amulētum aureum tenēns, ad
fontem prōcessit.
senex manūs ad caelum sustulit et
auxilium ā deā Sūle petīvit.

4 senex, deam precātus, amulētum
in fontem iniēcit et exiit.

5 fūr, quī amulētum aureum vīderat,
ad fontem revēnit.
fūr, ad fontem regressus, amulētum
in aquā quaesīvit.

6 fūr, amulētum adeptus, attonitus lēgit:

fūr amulētum dēiēcit et ē thermīs
perterritus fūgit.

Vilbia

Vilbia et Rubria, pōcula sordida lavantēs, in culīnā tabernae
garriēbant. hae puellae erant fīliae Latrōnis. Latrō, quī tabernam
tenēbat, erat vir magnae dīligentiae sed minimae prūdentiae.
Latrō, culīnam ingressus, puellās vituperāvit.

    'multa sunt pōcula sordida. iubeō vōs pōcula quam celerrimē   *5*
lavāre. labōrāte! nōlīte garrīre! loquāciōrēs estis quam psittacī.'

    Latrō, haec verba locūtus, exiit.

    Vilbia, tamen, quae pulchra et obstināta erat, patrī nōn pāruit.
pōcula nōn lāvit, sed Rubriae fībulam ostendit. Rubria fībulam,
quam soror tenēbat, avidē spectāvit.   *10*

Rubria:	quam pulchra, quam pretiōsa est haec fībula, mea Vilbia! eam īnspicere velim. quis tibi dedit? num argentea est?
Vilbia:	sānē argentea est. Modestus, mīles Rōmānus, eam mihi dedit. *15*
Rubria:	quālis est hic mīles? estne homō mendāx et ignāvus, sīcut cēterī mīlitēs Rōmānī?
Vilbia:	minimē! est vir maximae virtūtis. ōlim tria mīlia hostium occīdit. nunc lēgātum ipsum custōdit.
Rubria:	Herculēs alter est! ego autem tālem fābulam saepe ex *20* aliīs mīlitibus audīvī.
Vilbia:	cēterī mīlitēs mendācēs sunt, Modestus probus. simulac tabernam nostram intrāvit, eum statim amāvī. quantī erant umerī eius! quanta bracchia!
Rubria:	tibi favet fortūna, mea Vilbia. quid autem dē Bulbō *25* dīcis, quem ōlim amābās? tibi perīculōsum est Bulbum contemnere, quod rēs magicās intellegit.
Vilbia:	nōlī illam pestem commemorāre! Bulbus, saepe dē mātrimōniō locūtus, nihil umquam effēcit. sed Modestus, quī fortissimus et audācissimus est, mē *30* cūrāre potest. Modestus nunc est suspīrium meum.

dīligentiae: dīligentia
   industry, hard work
minimae: minimus *very little*
ingressus *having entered*
locūtus *having spoken*

fībulam: fībula *brooch*
avidē *eagerly*

quālis? *what sort of man?*

virtūtis: virtūs *courage*
tria mīlia *three thousand*
occīdit: occīdere *kill*
lēgātum: lēgātus *commander*
alter *another, a second*
autem *but*
quantī: quantus *how big*
bracchia *arms*

contemnere *reject, despise*

mātrimōniō: mātrimōnium
   marriage
suspīrium *heart-throb*

Modestus

Modestus et Strȳthiō ad tabernam Latrōnis ambulant. Strȳthiō, quamquam amīcus Modestī est, eum dērīdet.

Modestus:	ubi es, Strȳthiō? iubeō tē prope mē stāre.
Strȳthiō:	adsum. hercle! quam fortūnātus sum! prope virum summae virtūtis stō. tū enim fortior es quam Mārs ipse.
Modestus:	vērum dīcis. ōlim tria mīlia hostium occīdī.
Strȳthiō:	tē omnēs puellae amant, quod tam fortis et pulcher es. illa Vilbia, heri tē cōnspicāta, statim amāvit. multa dē tē rogāvit.
Modestus:	quid dīxit?
Strȳthiō:	mē avidē rogāvit, 'estne Herculēs?' 'minimē! est frāter eius', respondī. tum fībulam, quam puella alia tibi dederat, Vilbiae trādidī. 'Modestus, vir benignus et nōbilis', inquam, 'tibi hanc fībulam grātīs dat.' Vilbia, fībulam adepta, mihi respondit, 'quam pulcher Modestus est! quam līberālis! velim cum eō colloquium habēre.'
Modestus:	ēheu! nōnne molestae sunt puellae? mihi difficile est puellās vītāre. nimis pulcher sum.
Strȳthiō:	ecce! ad tabernam Latrōnis advēnimus. fortasse inest Vilbia, quae tē tamquam deum adōrat. *(tabernam intrant.)*

5   **Mārs** *Mars (god of war)*

vērum *the truth*

cōnspicāta: cōnspicātus
  having caught sight of

10

15   **inquam** *I said*
grātīs *free*
adepta: adeptus *having received, having obtained*
colloquium *talk, chat*
20   **nimis** *too*
inest: inesse *be inside*
tamquam *as, like*

Two silver brooches joined by a chain.

About the language 1: perfect active participles

1   In Stage 21, you met sentences containing perfect passive participles:

      rēx, ā Rōmānīs **honōrātus**, semper fidēlis manēbat.
      *The king, **having been honoured** by the Romans, always remained loyal.*

      puellae, ā patre **vituperātae**, nōn respondērunt.
      *The girls, **having been blamed** by their father, did not reply.*

2   In Stage 22, you have met the other kind of perfect participle. Study the way it is translated in the following examples:

      Vilbia, culīnam **ingressa**, sorōrī fībulam ostendit.
      *Vilbia, **having entered** the kitchen, showed the brooch to her sister.*

      senex, deam **precātus**, abiit.
      *The old man, **having prayed to** the goddess, went away.*

The words in **bold type** are perfect active participles. Like other participles they change their endings to agree with the nouns they describe. Compare the following pair of sentences:

singular	puer, mīlitēs **cōnspicātus**, valdē timēbat.
plural	puerī, mīlitēs **cōnspicātī**, valdē timēbant.

3   Translate the following examples:

a Modestus, tabernam ingressus, Vilbiam cōnspexit.
b Vilbia, multa verba locūta, tandem tacuit.
c mercātōrēs, pecūniam adeptī, ad nāvēs contendērunt.
d fēmina, deam Sūlem precāta, amulētum in fontem iniēcit.
e ancillae, ānulum cōnspicātae, eum īnspicere volēbant.

In each sentence, pick out the perfect active participle and the noun which it describes. State whether each pair is singular or plural.

4   Only a small group of verbs have a perfect active participle; they do not have a perfect passive participle.

amor omnia vincit

scaena prīma

Bulbus et amīcus in tabernā Latrōnis sunt. vīnum bibunt āleamque lūdunt. Bulbus amīcō multam pecūniam dēbet.

Gutta:	(*amīcus Bulbī*) quam īnfēlīx es! nōn sōlum puellam, sed etiam pecūniam āmīsistī.
Bulbus:	pecūniam nōn cūrō, sed Vilbiam meam āmittere nōlō.
Gutta:	quō modō eam retinēre potes? mīles Rōmānus, vir summae virtūtis, eam petit. heus! Venerem iactāvī! caupō! iubeō tē plūs vīnī ferre.

Bulbus: mīles, quī eam dēcēpit, homō mendāx ignāvusque est. Vilbia, ab eō dēcepta, nunc mē contemnit. eam saepe monuī, 'nōlī mīlitibus crēdere, praesertim Rōmānīs.' Vilbia tamen, hunc Modestum cōnspicāta, statim eum amāvit.

Gutta: puellīs nōn tūtum est per viās huius oppidī īre. tanta est arrogantia hōrum mīlitum. hercle! tū etiam īnfēlīcior es. canem iterum iactāvistī. alium dēnārium mihi dēbēs.

Bulbus: dēnārium libenter trādō, nōn puellam. ōdī istum mīlitem. Modestus tamen puellam retinēre nōn potest, quod auxilium ā deā petīvī. deam precātus, tabulam in fontem sacrum iniēcī. dīra imprecātiō, in tabulā scrīpta, iam in fonte deae iacet. (*intrant Modestus et Strȳthiō, quōs Bulbus nōn videt.*) mortem Modestī laetus exspectō.

Gutta: hercle! īnfēlīcissimus es. ecce! nōbīs appropinquat ipse Modestus. necesse est mihi quam celerrimē exīre.
(*exit currēns.*)

---

amor *love*
omnia *all, everything*

scaena *scene*

āleam … lūdunt *are playing dice*

Venerem: Venus *Venus (highest throw at dice)*
iactāvī: iactāre *throw*

praesertim *especially*

arrogantia *cheek, arrogance*
canem: canis *dog (lowest throw at dice)*

ōdī *I hate*

precātus *having prayed to*
tabulam: tabula *tablet*
imprecātiō *curse*
scrīpta: scrībere *write*

(line numbers: 5, 10, 15, 20, 25)

The Romans were very fond of games involving dice, both the kind we are used to (far left), and more novel varieties like the little man (left), who can fall six ways up; here he scores 2. The larger of the cubic dice has a hollow in it, presumably for loading the dice.

scaena secunda

Modestus īrātus Bulbum vituperat, quod verba eius audīvit.

Modestus:	quid dīcēbās, homuncule? mortem meam exspectās? asine! tū, quod mīlitem Rōmānum vituperāvistī, in magnō perīculō es. Strȳthiō! tē iubeō hanc pestem verberāre. tum ē tabernā ēice!	5

ēice: ēicere *throw out*

Strȳthiō invītus Bulbum verberāre incipit. Bulbus, fortiter sē dēfendēns, vīnum in caput Strȳthiōnis fundit. Modestus Bulbum, simulac tergum vertit, ferōciter pulsat. Bulbus exanimātus prōcumbit. Vilbia, quae clāmōrēs audīvit, intrat. ingressa, Bulbum humī iacentem videt et Modestum mollīre incipit. 10

incipit: incipere *begin*
fundit: fundere *pour*
tergum *back*
humī *on the ground*
mollīre *soothe*

Vilbia:	dēsine, mī Modeste. iste Bulbus, ā tē verberātus, iterum mē vexāre nōn potest. tū es leō, iste rīdiculus mūs. volō tē clēmentem esse et Bulbō parcere. placetne tibi?

clēmentem: clēmēns *merciful*

Modestus:	mihi placet. victōribus decōrum est victīs parcere. tē, nōn istum, quaerō.	15

victīs: victī *the conquered*
parcere *spare*

Vilbia:	ō Modeste, cūr mē ex omnibus puellīs ēlēgistī? quam laeta sum!
Modestus:	necesse est nōbīs in locō sēcrētō noctū convenīre.

sēcrētō: sēcrētus *secret*

Vilbia:	id facere nōn audeō. pater mē sōlam exīre nōn vult. ubi est hic locus?	20

noctū *by night*

Modestus:	prope fontem deae Sūlis. nōnne tibi persuādēre possum?

Vilbia:	mihi difficile est iussa patris neglegere, sed tibi resistere nōn possum.	25

iussa *orders, instructions*
neglegere *ignore, disregard*

Modestus:	dā mihi ōsculum.
Vilbia:	ēheu! ō suspīrium meum! mihi necesse est ad culīnam redīre, tibi noctem exspectāre.

exeunt. Bulbus, quī magnam partem huius colloquiī audīvit, surgit. quam celerrimē ēgressus, Guttam petit, cui cōnsilium callidum prōpōnit. 30

ēgressus *having gone out*
cui *to whom (dative of* quī*)*

scaena tertia

per silentium noctis thermās intrant Bulbus et Gutta. prope fontem
sacrum sē cēlant. Bulbus Guttae stolam et pallium, quod sēcum tulit,
ostendit.

Bulbus:	Gutta, volō tē haec vestīmenta induere. volō tē	
	persōnam Vilbiae agere. nōbīs necesse est dēcipere	5
	Modestum, quem brevī exspectō.	
Gutta:	vah! virō nōn decōrum est stolam gerere. praetereā	
	barbam habeō.	
Bulbus:	id minimī mōmentī est, quod in tenebrīs sumus.	
	nōnne tibi persuādēre possum? ecce! decem	10
	dēnāriōs tibi dō. nunc tacē! indue stolam	
	palliumque! stā prope fontem deae! ubi Modestus	
	fontī appropinquat, dīc eī verba suāvissima!	

Gutta, postquam stolam invītus induit, prope fontem stat. Modestus,
sōlus thermās ingressus, fontī appropinquat. 15

pallium *cloak*

vestīmenta *clothes*
persōnam Vilbiae agere *play*
the part of Vilbia
brevī *in a short time*
vah! *ugh!*
praetereā *besides*
mōmentī: mōmentum
importance
tenebrīs: tenebrae *darkness*

The reservoir of the spring as
it is today.

Modestus: Vilbia, mea Vilbia! Modestus, fortissimus mīlitum,
adest.
Gutta: ō dēliciae meae! venī ad mē.
Modestus: quam rauca est vōx tua! num lacrimās, quod tardus
adveniō?   *20*
Gutta: ita vērō! tam sollicita eram.
Modestus: lacrimās tuās siccāre possum. (*Modestus ad Guttam*   **siccāre** *dry*
advenit.) dī immortālēs! Vilbia! barbam habēs? quid
tibi accidit? ō!

tum Bulbus Modestum in fontem dēicit. Vilbia, thermās ingressa, ubi *25*
clāmōrēs audīvit, prope iānuam perterrita manet.

Modestus: pereō! pereō! parce! parce!
Bulbus: furcifer! Vilbiam meam, quam valdē amō, auferre   **auferre** *take away, steal*
audēs? nunc mihi facile est tē interficere.
Modestus: nōlī mē interficere. Vilbiam tibi reddō. eam ā tē   *30*
auferre nōlō. Vilbiam nōn amō.

Vilbia, simulatque haec audīvit, īrāta fontī appropinquat. Modestum
vituperāre incipit.

Vilbia: mē nōn amās? ō hominem ignāvum! ego ipsa tē
interficere velim.   *35*
Bulbus: mea Vilbia, victōribus decōrum est victīs parcere.
Vilbia: mī Bulbe, dēliciae meae, miserrima sum! longē   **longē errāvī: longē errāre**
errāvī.   *make a big mistake*
Bulbus: nōlī lacrimāre! ego tē cūrāre possum.
Vilbia: ō Bulbe! ō suspīrium meum!   *40*

Bulbus et Vilbia domum redeunt. Gutta stolam palliumque exuit.   **exuit: exuere** *take off*
dēnāriōs laetē numerat. Modestus ē fonte sē extrahit et madidus abit.

About the language 2: more about the genitive

1 In Book II you met examples of the genitive case like these:

> marītus **Galatēae** erat Aristō.
> *The husband **of Galatea** was Aristo.*

> prō templō **Caesaris** stat āra.
> *In front of the temple **of Caesar** stands an altar.*

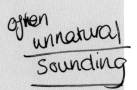
often unnatural sounding

2 In Stage 21 you have met another use of the genitive. Study the following examples:

satis pecūniae	*enough money*, literally, *enough of money*
nimium vīnī	*too much wine*
plūs sanguinis	*more blood*
multum cibī	*much food*

*of
of wine
of blood
of food*

Each phrase is made up of two words:

a A word like **plūs** or **nimium** indicating an amount or quantity.
b A noun in the genitive case.

3 Further examples:

a nimium pecūniae   **c** plūs labōris
b nihil perīculī   **d** multum aquae

partitive genitive

4 In Stage 22 you met examples like these:

> homō ingeniī prāvī   fēmina magnae dignitātis
> *a man of evil character*   *a woman of great prestige*

In both examples, a noun (**homō**, **fēmina**) is described by another noun and an adjective both in the genitive case. Such phrases can be translated in different ways. For example:

> puella magnae prūdentiae   vir summae virtūtis
> *a girl of great sense*   *a man of the utmost courage*
> Or, in more natural English: Or, in more natural English:
> *a very sensible girl*   *a very courageous man*

5 Further examples:

a homō minimae prūdentiae   **d** fābula huius modī
b iuvenis vīgintī annōrum   **e** puella maximae calliditātis
c fēmina magnae sapientiae   **f** vir ingeniī optimī

Word patterns: more adjectives and adverbs

In Stage 21 you met the following pattern:

1
adjectives		*adverbs*	
laetus	*happy*	laetē	*happily*
perītus	*skilful*	perītē	*skilfully*

2   Study another common pattern of adjectives and adverbs:

adjectives		*adverbs*	
brevis	*short*	brevi**ter**	*shortly*
ferōx	*fierce*	ferōci**ter**	*fiercely*

3   Using this pattern as a guide, complete the following table:

suāvis	*sweet*	suāviter	....
neglegēns	....	neglegenter	*carelessly*
audāx	....	audācter	....

4   Divide the following words into two lists, one of adjectives and one of adverbs. Then give the meaning of each word:

> fortis, fidēliter, īnsolēns, fortiter, sapienter, īnsolenter, fidēlis, sapiēns.

5   Choose the correct Latin word to translate the words in **bold type** in the following sentences:

   a   Quintus was a **sensible** young man. (prūdēns, prūdenter)
   b   Salvius rode **quickly** into the courtyard. (celer, celeriter)
   c   The soldier was **happy** because the goddess had cured him. (laetus, laetē)
   d   Vilbia worked **diligently** only when her father was watching. (dīligēns, dīligenter)
   e   Salvius sometimes acted **very cruelly** to his slaves. (crūdēlissimus, crūdēlissimē)

Practising the language

1 Complete each sentence with the correct form of the noun. Then translate the sentence.

    a Modestus per viās . . . . ambulābat, puellam quaerēns. (oppidī, oppidō)

    b Gutta, vir benignus, auxilium . . . . saepe dabat. (amīcī, amīcō)

    c Rubria, quae in tabernā labōrābat, ... vīnum obtulit. (iuvenis, iuvenī)

    d prope vīllam . . . . , turba ingēns conveniēbat. (haruspicis, haruspicī)

    e tabernārius . . . . multās rēs pretiōsās ostendit. (ancillārum, ancillīs)

    f clāmōrēs . . . . architectum vexāvērunt. (fabrōrum, fabrīs)

    g centuriō gladiōs hastāsque . . . . īnspicere coepit. (mīlitum, mīlitibus)

    h caupō vīnum pessimum . . . . offerēbat. (hospitum, hospitibus)

2 Complete each sentence with the correct form of the adjective. Then translate the sentence.

    a subitō ancilla . . . . in ātrium irrūpit. (perterrita, perterritae)

    b rēx, postquam hoc audīvit, fabrōs . . . . dīmīsit. (fessum, fessōs)

    c senātor quī aderat iuvenēs . . . . laudāvit. (callidum, callidōs)

    d omnēs cīvēs nāvem . . . . spectābant. (sacram, sacrās)

    e ubi in magnō perīculō eram, amīcus . . . . mē servāvit. (fidēlis, fidēlēs)

    f 'in illā īnsulā', inquit senex, 'habitant multī virī . . . .' (ferōx, ferōcēs)

    g fēmina . . . . , quae in vīllā manēbat, fūrem superāvit. (fortis, fortem, fortēs)

    h cīvēs in viīs oppidī . . . . mīlitēs vidēre solēbant. (multus, multī, multōs)

Magic and curses

When Roman religious sites are excavated, archaeologists sometimes find small sheets of lead or pewter inscribed with curses. These are known as **dēfīxiōnēs** or curse tablets. Over three hundred have been found in Britain, many of them directed at thieves.

The method of putting a curse on someone was as follows. The name of the offender, if known, was written on the tablet, with details of the crime. Sometimes he (or the stolen object) was then 'dedicated' to a god, who was called on to punish the offender, usually in a very unpleasant way. The completed tablet was then fastened to a tomb with a long nail or folded up and thrown into a well or spring.

A defixio found in the sacred spring at Bath reads:

> Docilianus, son of Brucerus, to the most holy goddess Sulis. I curse him who has stolen my hooded cloak, whether man or woman, whether slave or free, that … the goddess Sulis inflict death upon … and not allow him sleep or children now or in the future, until he has brought my hooded cloak to the temple of her divinity.

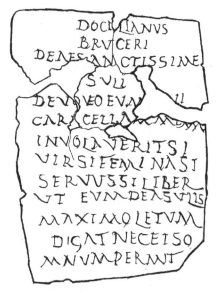

The first side of Docilianus' curse.

On another tablet a woman dedicates her stolen ring to the god Mars:

> Basilia gives to the temple of Mars her silver ring, that so long as someone, slave or free, keeps silent or knows anything about it, he may be accursed in his blood and eyes and every limb, or even have all his intestines entirely eaten away, if he has stolen the ring or been an accomplice.

One of the most famous tablets from Bath is the one that inspired the story about Vilbia and Modestus in this Stage:

> May he who has stolen Vilbia from me dissolve like water. May she who has devoured her be struck dumb, whether it be Velvinna or Exsupereus or Verianus … (here follows a list of six other suspects).

The Vilbia curse.

The Vilbia curse, like many others, was written backwards to increase the mystery of the process. Magic and apparently meaningless words like **bescu**, **berebescu**, **bazagra** were sometimes added to increase the effect, rather like the use of 'abracadabra' in spells. Sometimes we find a figure roughly drawn on the tablet, as in the illustration on p. 35. It depicts a bearded demon, carrying an urn and a torch, which were

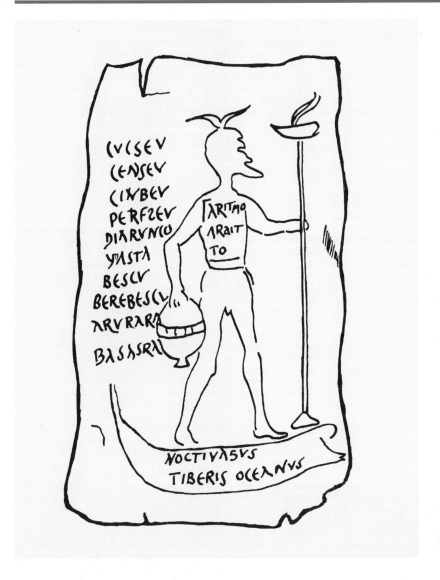

symbols of death. The boat in which he stands may represent the boat of Charon, the ferryman of the Underworld, who took the souls of the dead across the river Styx.

The wording of the curse can be very simple, just 'I dedicate' followed by the intended victim's name. But sometimes it can be ferociously eloquent, as in the following example:

> May burning fever seize all her limbs, kill her soul and her heart. O gods of the Underworld, break and smash her bones, choke her, let her body be twisted and shattered – phrix, phrox.

It may seem strange that religion should be used to bring harm to people in this very direct and spiteful way, but the Romans tended to see their gods as possible allies in the struggles of life. When they wished to injure an enemy, they thought it natural and proper to seek the gods' powerful help.

Vocabulary checklist 22

adeptus, adepta, adeptum	*having received, having obtained*
amor, amōris	*love*
caelum, caelī	*sky*
dēcipiō, dēcipere, dēcēpī, dēceptus	*deceive, fool*
ēligō, ēligere, ēlēgī, ēlēctus	*choose*
fundō, fundere, fūdī, fūsus	*pour*
hostis, hostis	*enemy*
iactō, iactāre, iactāvī, iactātus	*throw*
incipiō, incipere, incēpī, inceptus	*begin*
ingressus, ingressa, ingressum	*having entered*
lacrima, lacrimae	*tear*
minimus, minima, minimum	*very little, least*
moneō, monēre, monuī, monitus	*warn, advise*
nox, noctis	*night*
parcō, parcere, pepercī	*spare*
precātus, precāta, precātum	*having prayed (to)*
quantus, quanta, quantum	*how big*
quō modō?	*how? in what way?*
tūtus, tūta, tūtum	*safe*
verbum, verbī	*word*
virtūs, virtūtis	*courage*
vītō, vītāre, vītāvī, vītātus	*avoid*

One of the Bath curse tablets, folded as it was found.

HARUSPEX

STAGE 23

in thermīs

I

prope thermās erat templum, ā fabrīs Cogidubnī aedificātum.
rēx Cogidubnus cum multīs prīncipibus servīsque prō templō
sedēbat. Quīntus prope sellam rēgis stābat. rēgem prīncipēsque
manus mīlitum custōdiēbat. prō templō erat āra ingēns, quam
omnēs aspiciēbant. Memor, togam splendidam gerēns, prope   5
āram stābat.

duo sacerdōtēs, agnam nigram dūcentēs, ad āram
prōcessērunt. postquam rēx signum dedit, ūnus sacerdōs agnam
sacrificāvit. deinde Memor, quī iam tremēbat, alterī sacerdōtī,
'iubeō tē', inquit, 'ōmina īnspicere. dīc mihi: quid vidēs?'   10
sacerdos postquam iecur agnae īnspexit, anxius,
'iecur est līvidum', inquit. 'nōnne hoc mortem significat?
nōnne mortem virī clārī significat?'
Memor quī perterritus pallēscēbat, sacerdōtī respondit,
'minimē! dea Sūlis, quae precēs aegrōtōrum audīre solet,   15
nōbīs ōmina optima mīsit.'
haec verba locūtus, ad Cogidubnum sē vertit.
'ōmina sunt optima!' inquit. 'ōmina tibi remedium mīrābile
significant, quod dea Sūlis Minerva tibi favet.'
tum rēgem ac prīncipēs Memor in apodytērium dūxit.   20

manus mīlitum *a band of soldiers*
aspiciēbant: aspicere *look towards*
agnam: agna *lamb*
ōmina *omens (signs from the gods)*
iecur *liver*
līvidum: līvidus *lead-coloured*
significat: significāre *mean, indicate*
pallēscēbat: pallēscere *grow pale*
precēs: precum *prayers*
ac *and*

The altar at Bath. The base and the sculptured corner blocks are original; the rest of the Roman stone must have been re-used elsewhere during the Middle Ages. Compare the drawing opposite. At the top left of the photograph can be seen the stone statue base which is inscribed with Memor's name.

II

deinde omnēs in eam partem thermārum intrāvērunt, ubi
balneum maximum erat. Quīntus, prīncipēs secūtus,
circumspectāvit et attonitus,
    'hae thermae', inquit, 'maiōrēs sunt quam thermae
Pompēiānae!'   5
    servī cum magnā difficultāte Cogidubnum in balneum
dēmittere coepērunt. maximus clāmor erat. rēx prīncipibus
mandāta dabat. prīncipēs lībertōs suōs vituperābant, lībertī
servōs.
    tandem rēx ē balneō ēgressus, vestīmenta, quae servī   *10*
tulerant, induit. tum omnēs fontī sacrō appropinquāvērunt.
    Cephalus, quī anxius tremēbat, prope fontem stābat,
pōculum ōrnātissimum tenēns.
    'domine', inquit, 'pōculum aquae sacrae tibi offerō. aqua est
amāra, sed remedium potentissimum.'   *15*
    haec verba locūtus, rēgī pōculum obtulit. rēx pōculum ad
labra sustulit.
    subitō Quīntus, pōculum cōnspicātus, manum rēgis prēnsāvit
et clāmāvit,
    'nōlī bibere! hoc est pōculum venēnātum. pōculum huius   *20*
modī in urbe Alexandrīā vīdī. pōculum īnspicere volō. dā mihi!'

secūtus *having followed*

difficultāte: difficultās
   difficulty
dēmittere *let down, lower*

amāra: amārus *bitter*

labra *lips*
prēnsāvit: prēnsāre *take hold
   of, clutch*

tum pōculum Quīntus īnspicere coepit. Cephalus tamen
pōculum ē manibus Quīntī rapere temptābat. maxima pars
spectātōrum stābat immōta. sed Dumnorix, prīnceps
Rēgnēnsium, saeviēns pōculum rapuit et Cephalō obtulit. 25

'facile est nōbīs vērum cognōscere', clāmāvit. 'iubeō tē
pōculum haurīre. num aquam bibere timēs?'

Cephalus pōculum haurīre nōluit, et ad genua rēgis   **genua** *knees*
prōcubuit. rēx immōtus stābat. cēterī prīncipēs lībertum frūstrā
resistentem prēnsāvērunt. Cephalus, ā prīncipibus coāctus, 30   **coāctus: cōgere** *force, compel*
venēnum hausit. deinde, vehementer tremēns, gemitum
ingentem dedit et mortuus prōcubuit.

*This sculpture was placed over the entrance to the temple of Sulis
Minerva. It is a Celtic version of the Gorgon's head that Minerva wore
on her cloak or shield – a monster that could turn men to stone with a
glance.*

About the language 1: more about participles

1 In Stage 20 you met the present participle:

   > lībertus dominum **intrantem** vīdit.
   > *The freedman saw his master **entering**.*

2 In Stage 21 you met the perfect passive participle:

   > fabrī, ab architectō **laudātī**, dīligenter labōrābant.
   > *The craftsmen, (**having been**) **praised** by the architect, were working hard.*

3 In Stage 22 you met the perfect active participle:

   > Vilbia, thermās **ingressa**, clāmōrem audīvit.
   > *Vilbia, **having entered** the baths, heard a noise.*

4 Translate the following examples:

   a rēx, in mediā turbā sedēns, prīncipēs salūtāvit.
   b lībertus, in cubiculum regressus, Memorem excitāre temptāvit.
   c Vilbia fībulam, ā Modestō datam, Rubriae ostendit.
   d sacerdōtēs, deam precātī, agnam sacrificāvērunt.
   e templum, ā Rōmānīs aedificātum, prope fontem sacrum erat.
   f sorōrēs, in tabernā labōrantēs, mīlitem cōnspexērunt.
   g fūr rēs, in fontem iniectās, quaesīvit.
   h nōnnūllae ancillae, ā dominā verberātae, venēnum comparāvērunt.

   Pick out the noun and participle pair in each sentence and state whether
   the participle is present, perfect passive or perfect active.

5 In which of the sentences in paragraph 4 is the noun and participle pair
   singular and which plural?

epistula Cephalī

postquam Cephalus periit, servus eius rēgī epistulam trādidit, ā
Cephalō ipsō scrīptam:

    'rēx Cogidubne, in maximō perīculō es. Memor īnsānit.
mortem tuam cupit. iussit mē rem efficere. invītus Memorī
pāruī. fortasse mihi nōn crēdis. sed tōtam rem tibi nārrāre velim.   5

    ubi tū ad hās thermās advēnistī, remedium quaerēns, Memor
mē ad vīllam suam arcessīvit. vīllam ingressus, Memorem
perterritum invēnī.

    "Imperātor mortem Cogidubnī cupit", inquit. "iubeō tē hanc
rem administrāre. iubeō tē venēnum parāre. Cogidubnus enim   *10*
est homō ingeniī prāvī."

    Memorī respondī,

    "longē errās. Cogidubnus est vir ingeniī optimī. tālem rem
facere nōlō."

    Memor īrātus,   *15*

    "sceleste!" inquit. "lībertus meus es. mandāta mea facere
dēbēs. cūr mihi obstās?"

    rēx Cogidubne, diū recūsāvī obstinātus. diū beneficia tua
commemorāvī. tandem Memor custōdem arcessīvit, quī mē
verberāvit. ā custōde paene interfectus, Memorī tandem cessī.   *20*

    ad casam meam regressus, venēnum invītus parāvī. scrīpsī
tamen hanc epistulam et servō fidēlī trādidī. iussī servum tibi
epistulam trādere. veniam petō, quamquam facinus scelestum
parāvī. Memor coēgit mē hanc rem efficere. Memorem, nōn mē,
pūnīre dēbēs.'   *25*

īnsānit: īnsānīre *be mad, be
insane*

beneficia *acts of kindness,
favours*

regressus *having returned*

facinus *crime*
coēgit: cōgere *force, compel*

About the language 2: the plural of neuter nouns

1 You have now met the plural of neuter nouns like **templum** and **nōmen**:

  sunt multa **templa** in hāc urbe.
  There are many temples in this city.

  lībertus **nōmina** prīncipum recitāvit.
  The freedman read out the names of the chieftains.

2 Study the nominative and accusative forms of the following neuter nouns:

	2nd declension	3rd declension			
SINGULAR					
nominative	templum	nōmen	caput	vulnus	mare
accusative	templum	nōmen	caput	vulnus	mare
PLURAL					
nominative	templa	nōmina	capita	vulnera	maria
accusative	templa	nōmina	capita	vulnera	maria

3 Further examples:

  a aedificium erat splendidissimum.
  b ubi haec verba audīvit, Memor tacēbat.
  c medicus vulnus mīlitis īnspexit.
  d Cephalus cōnsilium subitō cēpit.
  e haec cubicula sunt sordidissima.
  f servī pōcula ad prīncipēs tulērunt.

subject

deficereish

Britannia perdomita

perdomita: perdomitus
conquered

When you have read this story, answer the questions at the end.

Salvius cum Memore anxius colloquium habet. servus ingressus ad Memorem currit.

servus:	domine, rēx Cogidubnus hūc venit. rēx togam splendidam ōrnāmentaque pretiōsa gerit. magnum numerum armātōrum sēcum dūcit.
Memor:	rēx armātōs hūc dūcit?
Salvius:	Cogidubnus, nōs suspicātus, ultiōnem petit. Memor, tibi necesse est mē adiuvāre. nōs enim Rōmānī sumus, Cogidubnus barbarus.

(intrat Cogidubnus. in manibus epistulam tenet, ā Cephalō scrīptam.)

Cogidubnus:	Memor, tū illās īnsidiās parāvistī. tū iussistī Cephalum venēnum comparāre et mē necāre. sed Cephalus, lībertus tuus, mihi omnia patefēcit.
Memor:	Cogidubne, id quod dīcis absurdum est. mortuus est Cephalus.
Cogidubnus:	Cephalus homō magnae prūdentiae erat. tibi nōn crēdidit. invītus tibi pāruit. simulac mandāta ista dedistī, scrīpsit Cephalus epistulam in quā omnia patefēcit. servus, ā Cephalō missus, epistulam mihi tulit.
Memor:	epistula falsa est, servus mendācissimus.
Cogidubnus:	tū, nōn servus, es mendāx. servus enim, multa tormenta passus, in eādem sententiā mānsit.
Salvius:	Cogidubne, cūr armātōs hūc dūxistī?
Cogidubnus:	Memorem ē cūrā thermārum iam dēmōvī.
Memor:	quid dīcis? tū mē dēmōvistī? innocēns sum.
Salvius:	rēx Cogidubne, quid fēcistī? tū, quī barbarus es, haruspicem Rōmānum dēmovēre audēs? tū, summōs honōrēs ā nōbīs adeptus, numquam contentus fuistī. nunc perfidiam apertē ostendis. Imperātor Domitiānus, arrogantiam tuam diū passus, ad mē epistulam nūper mīsit. in hāc epistulā iussit mē rēgnum tuum occupāre. iubeō tē igitur ad aulam statim redīre.
Cogidubnus:	ēn iūstitia Rōmāna! ēn fidēs! nūllī perfidiōrēs sunt quam Rōmānī. stultissimus fuī, quod Rōmānīs adhūc crēdidī. nunc, ā Rōmānīs dēceptus, ista ōrnāmenta, mihi ā Rōmānīs data, humī iaciō. Salvī, mitte nūntium ad Domitiānum: 'nōs tandem Cogidubnum vīcimus. Britannia perdomita est.'

(senex, haec locūtus, lentē per iānuam exit.)

armātōrum: armātī *armed men*

suspicātus *having suspected*
ultiōnem: ultiō *revenge*

5

10

īnsidiās: īnsidiae *trap, ambush*
patefēcit: patefacere *reveal*
absurdum: absurdus *absurd*

15

20

falsa: falsus *false, untrue*

tormenta *torture*
passus *having suffered*
eādem *the same*
sententiā: sententia *opinion*
dēmōvī: dēmovēre *dismiss*

25

30

perfidiam: perfidia *treachery*
apertē *openly*

rēgnum *kingdom*
occupāre *seize, take over*
ēn iūstitia! *so this is justice!*
fidēs *loyalty, trustworthiness*
perfidiōrēs: perfidus
    treacherous, untrustworthy
adhūc *up till now*
iaciō: iacere *throw*
vīcimus: vincere *conquer*

35

40

Questions

		Marks
1	Who is described as **anxius**?	1
2	Read what the slave says (lines 3–5). How do Memor and Salvius know from this that Cogidubnus' visit is not an ordinary one? Make two different points.	2
3	What is Salvius' explanation for Cogidubnus' visit (line 7)?	1
4	Why does Salvius think Memor should help him?	1
5	What accusation does Cogidubnus make against Memor (lines 12–13)?	3
6	Why is Memor certain that Cogidubnus is unable to prove his accusation (lines 15–16)?	1
7	What proof does Cogidubnus have? How did it come into his possession (lines 18–21)?	2
8	Why is Cogidubnus convinced that the slave is trustworthy?	1
9	What question does Salvius ask Cogidubnus?	1
10	Why do you think that he has remained silent up to this point?	1
11	In line 27, why is Memor upset?	1
12	In lines 29–31 Salvius accuses Cogidubnus of being ungrateful. What three points does he make?	3
13	What order does Salvius say he has received? Who has sent it (lines 32–4)?	2
14	**ista ōrnāmenta … humī iaciō** (lines 38–9). What is Cogidubnus doing when he says these words? Why do you think he does this?	2
15	How are the attitudes or situations of Memor, Salvius and Cogidubnus different at the end of this story from what they were at the beginning? Make one point about each character.	3

TOTAL **25**

Britannia perdomita,
on a Roman coin.

Word patterns: verbs and nouns

1   Study the form and meaning of the following verbs and nouns.

infinitive		perfect passive participle	noun	
pingere	*to paint*	pictus	pictor	*painter*
vincere	*to win*	victus	victor	*winner, victor*
līberāre	*to set free*	līberātus	līberātor	*liberator*

2   Using the pattern in paragraph 1 as a guide, complete the table below:

emere	*to buy*	ēmptus	ēmptor	. . . .
legere	. . . .	lēctus	. . . .	*reader*
spectāre	. . . .	spectātus	. . . .	. . . .

3   What do the following nouns mean:

   dēfēnsor, vēnditor, prōditor, amātor

4   Many English nouns ending in **-or** are derived from Latin verbs.
    Which verbs do the following English nouns come from? Use the
    Vocabulary to help you if necessary.

   demonstrator, curator, navigator, narrator, tractor, doctor

5   Can you suggest what the ending **-or** indicates in Latin and English?

Practising the language

1   Complete each sentence with the right word. Then translate the sentence.

   a   nōs ancillae fessae sumus; semper in vīllā . . . . (labōrāmus, labōrātis, labōrant)

   b   'quid faciunt illī servī?' 'pōcula ad mīlitēs . . . .' (ferimus, fertis, ferunt)

   c   fīlius meus vōbīs grātiās agere vult, quod mē . . . . (servāvimus, servāvistis, servāvērunt)

   d   quamquam prope āram . . . ., sacrificium vidēre nōn poterāmus. (stābāmus, stābātis, stābant)

   e   ubi prīncipēs fontī . . . ., Cephalus prōcessit, pōculum tenēns. (appropinquābāmus, appropinquābātis, appropinquābant)

   f   in maximō perīculō estis, quod fīlium rēgis . . . . (interfēcimus, interfēcistis, interfēcērunt)

   g   nōs, quī fontem sacrum numquam . . . ., ad thermās cum rēge īre cupiēbāmus. (vīderāmus, vīderātis, vīderant)

   h   dominī nostrī sunt benignī; nōbīs semper satis cibī . . . . (praebēmus, praebētis, praebent)

2   Complete each sentence with the most suitable perfect participle from the list below. Then translate the sentence.

   adeptus, locūtus, ingressus, missus, excitātus, superātus

   a   Cogidubnus, haec verba . . . ., ab aulā discessit.
   b   nūntius, ab amīcīs meīs . . . ., epistulam mihi trādidit.
   c   fūr, vīllam . . . ., cautē circumspectāvit.
   d   Bulbus, ā Modestō . . . ., sub mēnsā iacēbat.
   e   haruspex, ā Cephalō . . . ., ē lectō surrēxit.
   f   mīles, amulētum . . . ., in fontem iniēcit.

Roman religion

Sacrifices and presents to the gods

In this Stage Cogidubnus sacrificed a lamb to Sulis Minerva in the hope that the goddess would be pleased with his gift and would restore him to health. This was regarded as the right and proper thing to do in such circumstances. People in the ancient world thought that by offering animal sacrifices and other gifts to the gods they could keep on good terms with them and stand a better chance of getting their prayers answered. This was true at all levels of society. For example, if a general was going off to war, there would be a solemn public ceremony at which prayers and expensive sacrifices would be offered to the gods. Ordinary citizens would also offer sacrifices, hoping for a successful business deal, a safe voyage or the birth of a child; and in some Roman homes, to ensure the family's prosperity, offerings of food would be made to Vesta, the spirit of the hearth, and to the lares and penates, the spirits of the household and store cupboard.

   People also offered sacrifices and presents to the gods to honour them at their festivals, to thank them for some success or an escape from danger, or to keep a promise. For example, a cavalry officer stationed in the north of England set up an altar to the god Silvanus with this inscription:

> C. Tetius Veturius Micianus, captain of the Sebosian cavalry squadron, set this up as he promised to Silvanus the unconquered, in thanks for capturing a beautiful boar which many people before him tried to do but failed.

An emperor, as Chief Priest, leads a solemn procession. He covers his head with a fold of his toga. A bull, a sheep and a pig are to be sacrificed.

A model liver. Significant areas are labelled to help haruspices interpret any markings.

A haruspex examining a sacrificed bull.

Another inscription from a grateful woman in north Italy reads:

Tullia Superiana takes pleasure in keeping her promise to Minerva the unforgetting for giving her hair back.

Divination

A haruspex, like Memor, would be present at important sacrifices. He and his assistants would watch the way in which the victim fell; they would observe the smoke and flames when parts of the victim were placed on the altar fire; and, above all, they would cut the victim open and examine its entrails, especially the liver. They would look for anything unusual about the liver's size or shape, observe its colour and texture and note whether it had spots on its surface. They would then interpret what they saw and announce to the sacrificer whether the signs from the gods were favourable or not.

Such attempts to discover the future are known as divination. Another type of divination was performed by priests known as augurs who based their predictions on observations of the flight of birds. They would note the direction of flight, and observe whether the birds flew together or separately, what kind of birds they were and what noises they made.

In this sculpture of a sacrifice, notice the pipe-player, and the attendants with the decorated victim.

The Roman state religion

Religion in Rome and Italy included a bewildering variety of gods, demigods, spirits, rituals and ceremonies, whose origin and meaning was often a mystery to the worshippers themselves. The Roman state respected this variety but particularly promoted the worship of Jupiter and his family of gods and goddesses, especially Juno, Minerva, Ceres, Apollo, Diana, Mars and Venus. They were closely linked with their equivalent Greek deities, whose characteristics and colourful mythology were readily taken over by the Romans.

The rituals and ceremonies were organised by colleges of priests and other religious officials, many of whom were senators, and the festivals and sacrifices were carried out by them on behalf of the state. Salvius, for example, was a member of the Arval brotherhood, whose religious duties included praying for the emperor and his family. The emperor always held the position of **Pontifex Maximus** or Chief Priest. Great attention was paid to the details of worship. Everyone who watched the ceremonies had to stand quite still and silent, like Plancus in the Stage 17 story. Every word had to be pronounced correctly, otherwise the whole ceremony had to be restarted; a pipe-player was employed to drown noises and cries, which were thought to be unlucky for the ritual.

A priest's ritual headdress, from Roman Britain.

Left: *People kept little statues of their favourite gods in their homes, in small shrines. This model in Chester's Grosvenor Museum reconstructs a domestic shrine of Venus. The pipeclay statuette is original and would have been imported from Gaul (France).*

Above: *Often people promised to give something to the gods if they answered their prayers. Thus, Censorinus dedicated this thin silver plaque to Mars, in order to fulfil a vow.*

Three sculptures from Bath illustrate the mixture of British and Roman religion there.
Above: *A gilded bronze head of Sulis Minerva, presumably from her statue in the temple, shows the goddess as the Romans pictured her.*
Top right: *Nemetona and the horned Loucetius Mars.*
Right: *Three Celtic mother-goddesses.*

Religion and romanisation

The Roman state religion played an important part in the romanisation of the provinces of the empire. The Romans generally tolerated the religious beliefs and practices of their subject peoples unless they were thought to threaten their rule or their relationship with the gods which was so carefully fostered by sacrifices and correct rituals. They encouraged their subjects to identify their own gods with Roman gods who shared some of the same characteristics. We have seen at Bath how the Celtic Sulis and the Roman Minerva were merged into one goddess, Sulis Minerva, and how a temple was built in her honour in the Roman style. Another example is provided by an inscription recording the fulfilment of a promise made by a man called Peregrinus to Mars Loucetius and Nemetona. Here the Celtic god Loucetius has been linked to Mars, the Roman god of war.

Another feature of Roman religion which was intended to encourage acceptance of Roman rule was the worship of the emperor. In Rome itself, emperor worship was generally discouraged. However, the peoples of the eastern provinces of the Roman empire had always regarded their kings and rulers as divine, and were equally ready to pay divine honours to the Roman emperors. Gradually the Romans introduced this idea in the west as well. The Britons and other western peoples were encouraged to worship the **genius** (protecting spirit) of the emperor, linked with the goddess Roma. Altars were erected in honour of 'Rome and the emperor'. When an emperor died it was usual to deify him (make him a god), and temples were often built to honour the deified emperor in the provinces. One such temple, that of Claudius in Colchester, was destroyed by the British before it was even finished, during the revolt led by Queen Boudica in AD 60. The historian Tacitus tells us why:

> 'The temple dedicated to the deified Emperor Claudius seemed to the British a symbol of everlasting oppression, and the chosen priests used religion as an excuse for wasting British money.'

In general, however, the policy of promoting Roman religion and emperor worship proved successful in the provinces. Like other forms of romanisation it became popular with the upper and middle classes, who looked to Rome to promote their careers; it helped to make Roman rule acceptable, reduced the chance of uprisings and gave many people in the provinces a sense that they belonged to one great empire.

Emperor Augustus as Pontifex Maximus. In the provinces of the empire, the rulers were often worshipped, particularly after their death.

Vocabulary checklist 23

cēdō, cēdere, cessī	give in, give way
clārus, clāra, clārum	famous, distinguished
cōnspicātus, cōnspicāta, cōnspicātum	having caught sight of
cūra, cūrae	care
enim	for
gerō, gerere, gessī, gestus	wear
honor, honōris	honour, public position
iaciō, iacere, iēcī, iactus	throw
immōtus, immōta, immōtum	still, motionless
locūtus, locūta, locūtum	having spoken
mandātum, mandātī	instruction, order
modus, modī	manner, way, kind
nimium	too much
ōrnō, ōrnāre, ōrnāvī, ōrnātus	decorate
pāreō, pārēre, pāruī	obey
regressus, regressa, regressum	having returned
scio, scīre, scīvī	know
tālis, tāle	such
umquam	ever
venēnum, venēnī	poison

This bronze statuette represents a Romano-British worshipper bringing offerings to a god.

FUGA

STAGE 24

in itinere

Modestus et Strȳthiō, ex oppidō Aquīs Sūlis ēgressī, Dēvam
equitābant. in itinere ad flūmen altum vēnērunt, ubi erat pōns
sēmirutus. cum ad pontem vēnissent, equus trānsīre nōluit.

    'equus trānsīre timet', inquit Modestus. 'Strȳthiō, tū prīmus
trānsī!'

    cum Strȳthiō trānsiisset, equus trānsīre etiam tum nōlēbat.
Modestus igitur ex equō dēscendit. cum dēscendisset, equus
statim trānsiit.

    'eque! redī!' inquit Modestus. 'mē dēseruistī.'

    equus tamen in alterā rīpā immōtus stetit. Modestus
cautissimē trānsīre coepit. cum ad medium pontem vēnisset,
dēcidit pōns, dēcidit Modestus. mediīs ex undīs clāmāvit,

    'caudicēs, vōs pontem labefēcistis.'

Dēvam *to Chester*
altum: altus *deep*
sēmirutus *rickety*
cum *when*
5 **trānsīre** *cross*

10

labefēcistis: labefacere
   weaken

A stretch of Roman road that survives on Wheeldale Moor in North Yorkshire. This road is known as Wade's Causeway. In local legend, Wade was a giant who was said to have built the road by throwing stones at his wife.

Only the lower layers of road remain; the metalling has disappeared over the centuries (see page 66).

Quīntus cōnsilium capit

When you have read this story, answer the questions at the end.

cum Cogidubnus trīstis īrātusque ē vīllā Memoris exiisset,
Salvius quīnquāgintā mīlitēs arcessīvit. eōs iussit rēgem
prīncipēsque Rēgnēnsium comprehendere et in carcere retinēre.
hī mīlitēs, tōtum per oppidum missī, mox eōs invēnērunt.
Dumnorix tamen, ē manibus mīlitum noctū ēlāpsus, Quīntum   5
quaesīvit, quod eī crēdēbat.

cubiculum Quīntī ingressus, haec dīxit:

'amīce, tibi crēdere possum. adiuvā mē, adiuvā Cogidubnum.
paucīs Rōmānīs crēdō; plūrimī sunt perfidī. nēmō quidem
perfidior est quam iste Salvius quī Cogidubnum interficere   10
nūper temptāvit. nunc Cogidubnus, ā mīlitibus Salviī
comprehēnsus, in carcere iacet. rēx omnīnō dē vītā suā dēspērat.

'tū tamen es vir summae virtūtis magnaeque prūdentiae.
quamquam Salvius potentissimus est, nōlī rēgem, amīcum
tuum, dēserere. nōlī eum in carcere inclūsum relinquere. tū   15
anteā eum servāvistī. nōnne iterum servāre potes?'

cum Dumnorix haec dīxisset, Quīntus rem sēcum anxius
cōgitābat. auxilium Cogidubnō ferre volēbat, quod eum valdē
dīligēbat; sed rēs difficillima erat. subitō cōnsilium cēpit.

'nōlī dēspērāre!' inquit. 'rēgī auxilium ferre possumus. hanc   20
rem ad lēgātum Gnaeum Iūlium Agricolam clam referre
dēbēmus. itaque nōbīs festīnandum est ad ultimās partēs
Britanniae ubi Agricola bellum gerit. Agricola sōlus Salviō
obstāre potest, quod summam potestātem in Britanniā habet.
nunc nōbīs hinc effugiendum est.'   25

Dumnorix, cum haec audīvisset, cōnsilium audāx magnopere
laudāvit. tum Quīntus servum fidēlem arcessīvit, cui mandāta
dedit. servus exiit. mox regressus, cibum quīnque diērum
Quīntō et Dumnorigī trādidit. illī, ē vīllā ēlāpsī, equōs
cōnscendērunt et ad ultimās partēs īnsulae abiērunt.   30

comprehendere *arrest, seize*
carcere: carcer *prison*
ēlāpsus *having escaped*

quidem *indeed*

omnīnō *completely*

inclūsum: inclūsus *shut up,*
imprisoned
sēcum … cōgitābat *considered*
… to himself
dīligēbat: dīligere *be fond of*

nōbīs festīnandum est *we*
must hurry
ultimās: ultimus *furthest*
bellum gerit: bellum gerere
wage war, campaign
potestātem: potestās *power*
magnopere *greatly*
diērum: diēs *day*
cōnscendērunt: cōnscendere
mount, climb on

Questions

		Marks
1	**quīnquāgintā mīlitēs** (line 2). What orders did Salvius give them?	2
2	After Dumnorix escaped, why did he seek out Quintus? Which Latin word shows why he wasn't seen by the soldiers (lines 5–6)?	2
3	What did Dumnorix want Quintus to do?	1
4	What was Dumnorix's opinion of the Romans (line 9)?	1
5	**nēmō quidem perfidior est quam iste Salvius** (lines 9–10). Why did Dumnorix think this?	1
6	In lines 13–16 how did Dumnorix try to persuade Quintus? Make three points.	3
7	Why was Quintus willing to help Cogidubnus? What made him at first hesitate (lines 17–19)?	2
8	What did Quintus suggest to Dumnorix that they should do to help the king (lines 20–2)?	1
9	Where was Agricola and what was he doing?	2
10	Why did Quintus think that Agricola could block Salvius' plans?	1
11	In the preparations for travelling, what indicates that the journey was likely to be a long one (lines 27–9)?	1
12	In line 13 Quintus is described as **vir summae virtūtis magnaeque prūdentiae**. To what extent do you think this is a good or bad description? Support your answer with three examples taken from the story.	3

TOTAL **20**

About the language 1: cum and the pluperfect subjunctive

1   Study the following sentences:

cum Modestus ad pontem **advēnisset**, equus trānsīre nōlēbat.
*When Modestus **had arrived** at the bridge, the horse did not want to cross.*

cum servī omnia **parāvissent**, mercātor amīcōs in triclīnium dūxit.
*When the slaves **had prepared** everything, the merchant led his friends into the dining-room.*

The form of the verb in **bold type** is known as the subjunctive

2   The subjunctive is often used with the word **cum** meaning *when*, as in the examples above.

3   Further examples:

a   cum rēx exiisset, Salvius mīlitēs ad sē vocāvit.
b   cum gladiātōrēs leōnem interfēcissent, spectātōrēs plausērunt.
c   cum dominus haec mandāta dedisset, fabrī ad aulam rediērunt.
d   sorōrēs, cum culīnam intrāvissent, pōcula sordida lavāre coepērunt.

4   The examples of the subjunctive in paragraphs 1 and 3 are all in the same tense, the pluperfect subjunctive. Compare the 3rd person of the pluperfect subjunctive with the ordinary form of the pluperfect:

	PLUPERFECT	PLUPERFECT SUBJUNCTIVE	
	singular	*singular*	*plural*
first conjugation	portāverat	portāvisset	portāvissent
second conjugation	docuerat	docuisset	docuissent
third conjugation	trāxerat	trāxisset	trāxissent
fourth conjugation	dormīverat	dormīvisset	dormīvissent
irregular verbs			
esse (*to be*)	fuerat	fuisset	fuissent
velle (*to want*)	voluerat	voluisset	voluissent

Salvius cōnsilium cognōscit

[handwritten: author section islands]

postrīdiē, cum Quīntus et Dumnorix ad ultimās partēs īnsulae
contenderent, mīlitēs Dumnorigem per oppidum frūstrā
quaerēbant. rem dēnique Salviō nūntiāvērunt. ille, cum dē fugā
Dumnorigis cognōvisset, vehementer saeviēbat. tum Quīntum
quaesīvit; cum eum quoque nusquam invenīre potuisset,
Belimicum, prīncipem Canticōrum, arcessīvit.

'Belimice', inquit, 'iste Dumnorix ē manibus meīs effūgit;
abest quoque Quīntus Caecilius. neque Dumnorigī neque
Quīntō crēdō. ī nunc; dūc mīlitēs tēcum; illōs quaere in omnibus
partibus oppidī. quaere servōs quoque eōrum. facile est nōbīs
servōs torquēre et vērum ita cognōscere.'

Belimicus, multīs cum mīlitibus ēgressus, per oppidum
dīligenter quaerēbat. intereā Salvius anxius reditum eius
exspectābat. cum Salvius rem sēcum cōgitāret, Belimicus subitō
rediit exsultāns. servum Quīntī in medium ātrium trāxit.

Salvius ad servum trementem conversus,

'ubi est Quīntus Caecilius?' inquit. 'quō fūgit Dumnorix?'

'nescio', inquit servus quī, multa tormenta passus, vix
quicquam dīcere poterat. 'nihil scio', iterum inquit.

Belimicus, cum haec audīvisset, gladium dēstrictum ad
iugulum servī tenuit.

'melius est tibi', inquit, 'vērum Salviō dīcere.'

fugā: fuga *escape*

5 **nusquam** *nowhere*

ī: īre *go*

10 **torquēre** *torture*

[handwritten: 11, 12]

reditum: reditus *return*

15 **exsultāns: exsultāre** *exult, be*
16 *triumphant*
conversus *having turned*

quicquam *anything*
20 **dēstrictum: dēstringere** *draw*
iugulum *throat*

[handwritten: nusquam: nowhere]

servus quī iam dē vītā suā dēspērābat,
      'cibum quīnque diērum tantum parāvī', inquit susurrāns.
'nihil aliud fēcī. dominus meus cum Dumnorige in ultimās   25
partēs Britanniae discessit.'
      Salvius 'hercle!' inquit. 'ad Agricolam iērunt. Quīntus, ā
Dumnorige incitātus, mihi obstāre temptat; homō tamen
magnae stultitiae est; mihi resistere nōn potest, quod ego   **stultitiae: stultitia** *stupidity*
maiōrem auctōritātem habeō quam ille.'   30
      Salvius, cum haec dīxisset, Belimicō mandāta dedit. eum
iussit cum trīgintā equitibus exīre et fugitīvōs comprehendere.   **fugitīvōs: fugitīvus** *fugitive*
servum carnificibus trādidit. deinde scrībam arcessīvit cui   **scrībam: scrība** *scribe,*
epistulam dictāvit. ūnum ē servīs suīs iussit hanc epistulam   *secretary*
quam celerrimē ad Agricolam ferre.   35
      intereā Belimicus, Quīntum et Dumnorigem per trēs diēs
secūtus, eōs tandem in silvā invēnit. equitēs statim impetum in
eōs fēcērunt. amīcī, ab equitibus circumventī, fortiter resistēbant.
dēnique Dumnorix humī cecidit mortuus. cum equitēs corpus   **cecidit: cadere** *fall*
Dumnorigis īnspicerent, Quīntus, graviter vulnerātus, magnā   40   **corpus** *body*
cum difficultāte effūgit.

Aerial view of Shropshire section of the Roman road followed by
Quintus and Dumnorix to Chester.

About the language 2: cum and the imperfect subjunctive

1 In this Stage, you have met sentences with **cum** and the pluperfect subjunctive.

> senex, cum pecūniam **invēnisset**, ad vīllam laetus rediit.
> *When the old man **had found** the money, he returned happily to the villa.*

> cum rem **cōnfēcissent**, abiērunt.
> *When they **had finished** the job, they went away.*

2 Now study the following examples:

> cum custōdēs **dormīrent**, fūrēs ē carcere effūgērunt.
> *When the guards **were sleeping**, the thieves escaped from the prison.*

> Modestus, cum in Britanniā **mīlitāret**, multās puellās amābat.
> *When Modestus **was serving in the army** in Britain, he loved many girls.*

In these sentences, **cum** is being used with a different tense of the subjunctive, the imperfect subjunctive

3 Further examples:

a cum hospitēs cēnam cōnsūmerent, fūr cubiculum intrāvit.
b cum prīnceps rem cōgitāret, nūntiī subitō revēnērunt.
c iuvenēs, cum bēstiās agitārent, mīlitem vulnerātum cōnspexērunt.
d puella, cum epistulam scrīberet, sonitum mīrābilem audīvit.

4 Compare the 3rd person of the imperfect subjunctive with the infinitive:

	INFINITIVE	IMPERFECT SUBJUNCTIVE	
		singular	*plural*
first conjugation	portāre	portāret	portārent
second conjugation	docēre	docēret	docērent
third conjugation	trahere	traheret	traherent
fourth conjugation	audīre	audīret	audīrent
irregular verbs			
	esse	esset	essent
	velle	vellet	vellent

Word patterns: opposites

1   You have already met the following opposites:

volō	*I want*	nōlō	*I do not want*
scio	*I know*	nescio	*I do not know*

Study the words on the left of the table and find their opposites on the right. Then fill in their meanings.

umquam	*ever*	nēmō	....
homō	*man*	nusquam	....
usquam	*anywhere*	negōtium	....
ōtium	*leisure*	numquam	....

2   Study these further ways of forming opposites and give the meanings of the words on the right:

patiēns	*patient*	impatiēns	....
ūtilis	*useful*	inūtilis	....
cōnsentīre	*to agree*	dissentīre	....
facilis	*easy*	difficilis	....

3   From the box choose the correct Latin words to translate the words in **bold type** in the following sentences:

sānus	fēlīx	similis	inimīcus
dissimilis	īnsānus	amīcus	īnfēlīx

    a   A black cat was thought to be **lucky** but a stumble was **unlucky**.
    b   Bulbus must be **mad** to love Vilbia.
    c   Strythio is the **friend** of Modestus, but Bulbus is his **enemy**.
    d   Vilbia is **like** her sister in looks, but **different** in character.

4   Work out the meanings of the following words:

      immōtus, incertus, dissuādeō, incrēdibilis, nocēns, ignōtus.

Practising the language

1 Complete each sentence with the correct form of the adjective. Then translate the sentence.

    a medicus puellae . . . . pōculum dedit. (aegram, aegrae)
    b hospitēs coquum . . . . laudāvērunt. (callidum, callidō)
    c faber mercātōrī . . . . dēnāriōs reddidit. (īrātum, īrātō)
    d ancillae dominō . . . . pārēre nōlēbant. (crūdēlem, crūdēlī)
    e centuriō mīlitēs . . . . vituperābat. (ignāvōs, ignāvīs)
    f puer stultus nautīs . . . . crēdidit. (mendācēs, mendācibus)
    g stolās . . . . emēbat fēmina. (novās, novīs)
    h . . . . amīcīs pecūniam obtulī. (omnēs, omnibus)

2 With the help of paragraph 3 on p. 153 in the Language Information section, replace the words in **bold type** with the correct form of the pronoun **is**. Then translate the sentence. For example:

    Rūfilla in hortō ambulābat. Quīntus **Rūfillam** salūtāvit.
    This becomes:
    Rūfilla in hortō ambulābat. Quīntus **eam** salūtāvit.
    *Rufilla was walking in the garden. Quintus greeted **her**.*

In sentences **g** and **h**, you may need to look up the gender of a noun in the Vocabulary at the end of the book.

    a Quīntus mox ad aulam advēnit. ancilla **Quīntum** in ātrium dūxit.
    b Salvius in lectō recumbēbat. puer **Salviō** plūs cibī obtulit.
    c Rūfilla laetissima erat; marītus **Rūfillae** tamen nōn erat contentus.
    d Britannī ferōciter pugnāvērunt, sed Rōmānī tandem **Britannōs** vīcērunt.
    e barbarī impetum in nōs fēcērunt. **barbarīs** autem restitimus.
    f multae fēminae prō templō conveniēbant. līberī **fēminārum** quoque aderant.
    g prope templum est fōns sacer; **fontem** saepe vīsitāvī.
    h in oppidō Aquīs Sūlis erant thermae maximae; architectus Rōmānus **thermās** exstrūxit.

Travel and communication

Judged by modern standards, travelling in the Roman world was neither easy nor comfortable; nevertheless, people travelled extensively and there was much movement of goods throughout the provinces of the empire. This was made possible by a remarkable network of straight, well-surfaced roads which connected all major towns by the shortest possible routes. Travellers walked, used carriages or carts, or rode, generally on mules or ponies. Horses were ridden mainly by cavalrymen or government officials. Journey times were affected by many factors; for example, the freshness of animals and travellers, the time of year and the gradients of the road. In good conditions a traveller might cover 20 miles on foot, 25–30 miles by carriage, perhaps a little more by mule.

The line of a Roman road was first laid out by surveyors. By taking sightings from high points using smoke from fires, it was possible to ensure that each section of road took the shortest practicable route between the points. River valleys and impassable mountains forced the surveyors to make diversions, but once past the obstructions, the roads usually continued along their original line. After the line had been chosen, an embankment of earth, called an **agger**, was raised to act as a firm foundation. An agger could be as high as 1.2–1.5 metres. In this was embedded a footing of large stones. This was covered with a layer of smaller stones, rubble and hardcore, and the surface was faced with local materials: large flat stones, small flints or slag from iron mines. This final surface is known as metalling and was curved or 'cambered' to provide effective drainage. On either side of the agger, ditches were dug for the same purpose.

Rubble layer and kerbstones at Wheeldale Moor - see also page 57.

Metalling with large flat stones: the Appian Way at Minturnae, Italy.

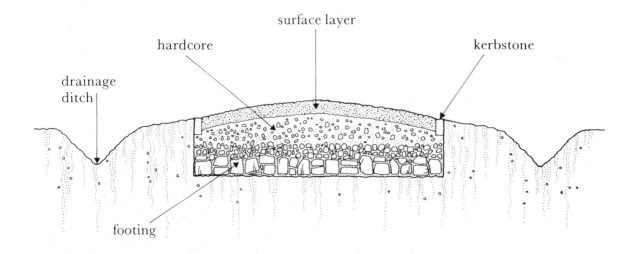

Roman road-building was generally carried out with great skill and thoroughness, and was not equalled in Britain until the nineteenth century when J. L. McAdam devised a road surface of small cut stones. Many modern roads still follow the Roman routes and these can be seen very clearly on Ordnance Survey maps.

Three forms of transport: a light carriage with two horses, passing a milestone; an enclosed coach of the Imperial Post with seating inside and on top, drawn by two mules; and an agricultural wagon carrying a skin full of wine, drawn by two eager oxen.

The roads' original purpose was to allow rapid movement of Roman troops and so ensure military control of the provinces. Other travellers included Roman government officials, who made use of a system known as the Imperial Post (**cursus pūblicus**). A traveller with a government warrant (**diplōma**) who was making a journey on official business was supplied with fresh horses at posting stations which were sited at frequent intervals along all main roads; every effort was made to speed such a traveller on his way. In particular, the cursus publicus was used for carrying government correspondence. It has been estimated that an official courier could average 50 miles a day; in an emergency, by travelling night and day, he could treble this distance. Private letters carried by a person's own slave took much longer.

A traveller in a hooded cloak, from a relief. An inscription found with it shows that he is paying the innkeeper's wife for a meal for himself and his mule.

Travellers would break long journeys with overnight stays at roadside inns. These were, for the most part, small, dirty and uncomfortable, and were frequented by thieves, prostitutes and drunks. The innkeepers, too, were often dishonest. Wealthy travellers would try to avoid using these inns by arranging to stay with friends or acquaintances, where possible.

Travelling by sea was generally more popular, although it was restricted to the sailing season (March to November) and was fraught with danger from pirates, storms and shipwrecks. Most sea journeys were undertaken on merchant ships; passenger shipping as we know it did not exist, except for the occasional ferry. A traveller would have to wait until a merchant ship was about to put to sea and bargain with the captain for an acceptable fare.

The ship would not set sail until the winds were favourable and an animal had been sacrificed to the gods. There were also certain days which were considered unlucky, rather like our Friday 13th, when no ship would leave port. When at last all was ready, the passenger would come on board with his slaves, bringing enough food and wine to last them until the next port of call. No cabins were provided, except for the very wealthy, and passengers would sleep on deck, perhaps in a small portable shelter, which would be taken down during the day.

When the ship came safely to port, the captain would thank the gods by making another sacrifice on board. Then a tugboat, manned by rowers, would tow the ship to her berth at the quayside.

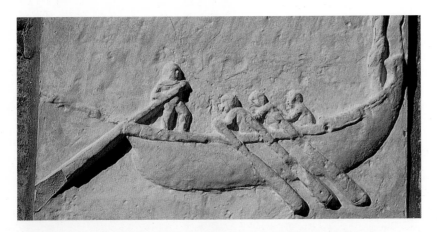

A tugboat.

A merchant ship in a harbour. On the left is a lighthouse approached by a causeway. The stern of the ship can be seen, with a carved swan's head, one of the large oars used for steering, and a small cabin.

Vocabulary checklist 24

auctōritās, auctōritātis — authority
audāx, *gen.* audācis — bold, daring
carcer, carceris — prison
comprehendō, comprehendere,
  comprehendī, comprehēnsus — arrest, seize
cum — when
dēserō, dēserere, dēseruī, dēsertus — desert
ēgressus, ēgressa, ēgressum — having gone out
eques, equitis — horseman
flūmen, flūminis — river
humī — on the ground
intereā — meanwhile
maximē — very greatly,
    most of all

neque ... neque — neither ... nor
oppugnō, oppugnāre, oppugnāvī,
  oppugnātus — attack
passus, passa, passum — having suffered
patefaciō, patefacere, patefēcī,
  patefactus — reveal
pōns, pontis — bridge
trānseō, trānsīre, trānsiī — cross
trīstis, trīste — sad
vērum, vērī — the truth

A Roman milestone.

MILITES

STAGE 25

Dēvae

1 mīles legiōnis secundae per castra ambulābat. subitō
iuvenem ignōtum prope horreum latentem cōnspexit.
    'heus tū', clāmāvit mīles, 'quis es?'
    iuvenis nihil respondit. mīles iuvenem iterum rogāvit quis
esset. iuvenis fūgit.

2 mīles iuvenem petīvit et facile superāvit.
    'furcifer!' exclāmāvit. 'quid prope horreum facis?'
    iuvenis dīcere nōlēbat quid prope horreum faceret. mīles
eum ad centuriōnem dūxit.

3 centuriō, iuvenem cōnspicātus,
    'hunc agnōscō!' inquit. 'explōrātor Britannicus est, quem
saepe prope castra cōnspexī. quō modō eum cēpistī?'
    tum mīles explicāvit quō modō iuvenem cēpisset.

4 centuriō, ad iuvenem conversus,
    'cūr in castra vēnistī?' rogāvit.
    iuvenis tamen tacēbat. centuriō, ubi cognōscere nōn
poterat cūr iuvenis in castra vēnisset, mīlitem iussit eum ad
carcerem dūcere.

    iuvenis, postquam verba centuriōnis audīvit,
    'ego sum Vercobrix', inquit, 'fīlius prīncipis
Deceanglōrum. vōbīs nōn decōrum est mē in carcere tenēre.'
    'fīlius prīncipis Deceanglōrum?' exclāmāvit centuriō.
'libentissimē tē videō. nōs tē diū quaerimus, cellamque
optimam tibi in carcere parāvimus.'

Strȳthiō

optiō per castra ambulat. Strȳthiōnem, iam Dēvam regressum, cōnspicit.

optiō: heus Strȳthiō! hūc venī! tibi aliquid dīcere volō.

Strȳthiō: nōlī mē vexāre! occupātus sum. Modestum quaerō, quod puella eum exspectat.   *5*

optiō: mī Strȳthiō, quamquam occupātissimus es, dēbēs maximā cum dīligentiā mē audīre. centuriō tē iubet ad carcerem statim festīnāre.

Strȳthiō: īnsānit centuriō! innocēns sum.

optiō: tacē! centuriō Modestum quoque iussit ad carcerem *10*
festīnāre.

Strȳthiō: deōs testēs faciō. innocentēs sumus. nūllum facinus commīsimus.

optiō: caudex! tacē! centuriō vōs ambōs carcerem custōdīre iussit.   *15*

Strȳthiō: nōlī mē vituperāre! rem nunc intellegō! centuriō nōs vult custōdēs carceris esse. decōrum est centuriōnī nōs ēligere, quod fortissimī sumus.

optiō: *(susurrāns)* difficile est mihi hoc crēdere.

Strȳthiō: quid dīcis?   *20*

optiō: quamquam fortissimī estis, dīligentiam quoque maximam praestāre dēbētis. nam inter captīvōs est Vercobrix, iuvenis magnae dignitātis, cuius pater est prīnceps Deceanglōrum. necesse est vōbīs Vercobrigem dīligentissimē custōdīre.   *25*

Strȳthiō: nōlī anxius esse, mī optiō. nōbīs nihil difficile est, quod fortissimī sumus, ut anteā dīxī. ego et Modestus, cum in Āfricā mīlitārēmus, nōn ūnum hominem, sed tōtam prōvinciam custōdiēbāmus.

exeunt. optiō centuriōnem quaerit, Strȳthiō amīcum.   *30*

optiō *optio (military officer, ranking below centurion)*
castra *camp*

commīsimus: committere *commit*
ambōs: ambō *both*

praestāre *show, display*
captīvōs: captīvus *prisoner, captive*
cuius *whose (genitive of* **quī***)*
prōvinciam: prōvincia *province*

Tombstone of an optio, from Chester (a copy with the painting re-created).

Modestus custōs

Modestus et Strȳthiō, carcerem ingressī, cellās in quibus captīvī erant īnspiciēbant. habēbat Strȳthiō tabulam in quā nōmina captīvōrum scrīpta erant. Modestus eum rogāvit in quā cellā Vercobrix inclūsus esset. Strȳthiō, tabulam īnspiciēns, cognōvit ubi Vercobrix iacēret, et Modestum ad cellam dūxit. Modestus, 5 cum ad portam cellae advēnisset, incertus cōnstitit.

    Strȳthiō 'cūr cellam intrāre timēs?' inquit. 'vīnctus est fīlius prīncipis Deceanglōrum. tē laedere nōn potest.'

    cum Strȳthiō haec dīxisset, Modestus īrātus exclāmāvit, 'caudex, prīncipis fīlium nōn timeō! cōnstitī quod tē 10 exspectābam. volō tē mihi portam aperīre!'

    cum portam Strȳthiō aperuisset, Modestus rūrsus haesitāvit.

    'obscūra est cella', inquit Modestus anxius. 'fer mihi lucernam.'

    Strȳthiō, vir summae patientiae, lucernam tulit amīcōque 15 trādidit. ille, cellam ingressus, ē cōnspectū discessit.

    in angulō cellae iacēbat Vercobrix. Modestus, cum eum vīdisset, gladium dēstrīnxit. tum, ad mediam cellam prōgressus, Vercobrigem vituperāre coepit. Vercobrix tamen contumēliās Modestī audīre nōn poterat, quod graviter dormiēbat. 20

    subitō arānea, ē tēctō cellae lāpsa, in nāsum Modestī incidit et trāns ōs cucurrit. Modestus, ab arāneā territus, ē cellā fūgit, vehementer clāmāns.

    Strȳthiō, quī extrā cellam stābat, attonitus erat. nesciēbat enim cūr Modestus clāmāret. 25

    'Strȳthiō! Strȳthiō!' clāmāvit Modestus. 'claude portam cellae. nōbīs necesse est summā cum dīligentiā Vercobrigem custōdīre. etiam arāneae eum adiuvant!'

    Strȳthiō, cum portam clausisset, Modestum territum rogāvit quid accidisset. 30

    'Modeste', inquit, 'quam pallidus es! num captīvum timēs?'

    'minimē! pallidus sum, quod nōn cēnāvī', respondit.

    'vīsne mē ad culīnam īre et tibi cēnam ferre?' rogāvit Strȳthiō.

    'optimum cōnsilium est!' inquit alter. 'tū tamen hīc manē. melius est mihi ipsī ad culīnam īre, quod coquus decem dēnāriōs 35 mihi dēbet.'

    haec locūtus, ad culīnam statim cucurrit.

---

cellās: cella *cell*
tabulam: tabula *writing tablet*

incertus: *uncertain*
cōnstitit: cōnsistere *halt, stop*
vīnctus: vincīre *bind, tie up*

haesitāvit: haesitāre *hesitate*
obscūra: obscūrus *dark, gloomy*
lucernam: lucerna *lamp*
patientiae: patientia *patience*
cōnspectū: cōnspectus *sight*
angulō: angulus *corner*
prōgressus *having advanced*
contumēliās: contumēlia *insult, abuse*
arānea *spider*
tēctō: tēctum *ceiling, roof*
lāpsa: lāpsus *having fallen*
trāns *across*
ōs *face*

pallidus *pale*

hīc *here*

About the language 1: indirect questions

1   In Book I, you met sentences like this:

'quis clāmōrem audīvit?'   'ubi habitat rēx?'
'*Who heard the shout?*'   '*Where does the king live?*'

In each example, a question is being *asked*. These examples are known as direct questions

2   In Stage 25, you have met sentences like this:

centuriō nesciēbat **quis clāmōrem audīvisset**.
*The centurion did not know **who had heard the shout**.*

equitēs cognōvērunt **ubi rēx habitāret**.
*The horsemen found out **where the king was living**.*

In each of these examples, the question is referred to, but not asked directly. These examples are known as indirect questions. The verb in an indirect question in Latin is subjunctive.

3   Compare the following examples:

direct questions	*indirect questions*
'quid Vercobrix fēcit?'	mīlitēs intellēxērunt quid Vercobrix fēcisset.
'*What has Vercobrix done?*'	*The soldiers understood what Vercobrix had done.*
'quis appropinquat?'	custōs nesciēbat quis appropinquāret.
'*Who is approaching?*'	*The guard did not know who was approaching.*
'ubi sunt barbarī?'	Rōmānī cognōvērunt ubi barbarī essent.
'*Where are the barbarians?*'	*The Romans found out where the barbarians were.*

4   Further examples of direct and indirect questions:

a   'quis puerum interfēcit?'
b   nēmō sciēbat quis puerum interfēcisset.
c   'ubi pecūniam invēnērunt?'
d   iūdex mē rogāvit ubi pecūniam invēnissent.
e   Salvius nesciēbat cūr Quīntus rēgem adiuvāret.
f   Cogidubnus cognōvit quō modō Cephalus venēnum comparāvisset.
g   Quīntus scīre voluit quid in templō esset.
h   Salvius tandem intellēxit quō Quīntus et Dumnorix fūgerent.

In each of the *indirect* questions state whether the subjunctive is imperfect or pluperfect.

Modestus perfuga

perfuga *deserter*

I

Modestus, ēgressus ē culīnā ubi cēnam optimam cōnsūmpserat,
ad carcerem lentē redībat.

    ubi carcerī appropinquāvit, portam apertam vīdit. permōtus,
'dī immortālēs!' inquit. 'Strȳthiō, num portam carceris
apertam relīquistī? nēminem neglegentiōrem quam tē nōvī.'   5

    carcerem ingressus, portās omnium cellārum apertās invēnit.
cum hoc vīdisset,

    'ēheu!' inquit. 'omnēs portae apertae sunt! captīvī, ē cellīs
ēlāpsī, omnēs fūgērunt!'

    Modestus rem anxius cōgitāvit. nesciēbat enim quō captīvī   10
fūgissent; intellegere nōn poterat cūr Strȳthiō abesset.

    'quid facere dēbeō? perīculōsum est hīc manēre ubi mē
centuriō invenīre potest. mihi fugiendum est. ō Strȳthiō,
Strȳthiō! coēgistī mē statiōnem dēserere. mē perfugam fēcistī.
sed deōs testēs faciō. invītus statiōnem dēserō.'   15

permōtus *alarmed, disturbed*

mihi fugiendum est *I must flee*
statiōnem: statiō *post*

II

Modestus, haec locūtus, subitō sonitum audīvit. aliquis portam
cellae Vercobrigis aperīre et exīre temptābat!

    'mihi ē carcere fugiendum est', aliquis ē cellā clāmāvit.

    Modestus, cum haec audīvisset, ad portam cellae cucurrit et
clausit.   *5*

    'Vercobrix, tibi in cellā manendum est!' clāmāvit Modestus.
'euge! nōn effūgit Vercobrix! eum captīvum habeō! euge! nunc
mihi centuriō nocēre nōn potest, quod captīvum summae
dignitātis in carcere retinuī.'

    Modestus autem anxius manēbat; nesciēbat enim quid
Strȳthiōnī accidisset. subitō pugiōnem humī relictum cōnspexit.

    'heus, quid est? hunc pugiōnem agnōscō! est pugiō
Strȳthiōnis! Strȳthiōnī dedī, ubi diem nātālem celebrābat. ēheu!
cruentus est pugiō. ō mī Strȳthiō! nunc rem intellegō. mortuus
es! captīvī, ē cellīs ēlāpsī, tē necāvērunt. ēheu! cum ego tuam
cēnam in culīnā cōnsūmerem, illī tēcum pugnābant! ō Strȳthiō!
nēmō īnfēlīcior est quam ego. nam tē amābam sīcut pater fīlium.
Vercobrix, quī in hāc cellā etiam nunc manet, poenās dare dēbet.
heus! Vercobrix, mē audī! tibi moriendum est, quod Strȳthiō
meus mortuus est.'

aliquis someone

nocēre harm

relictum: relinquere leave

cruentus covered in blood

tibi moriendum est you must
   die

10

15

20

III

Modestus in cellam furēns irrumpit. captīvum, quī intus latet,
verberāre incipit.

captīvus:	Modeste! mī Modeste! dēsine mē verberāre! nōnne mē agnōscis? Strȳthiō sum, quem tū amās sīcut pater fīlium.
Modestus:	Strȳthiō? Strȳthiō! num vīvus es? cūr vīvus es? sceleste! furcifer! ubi sunt captīvī quōs custōdiēbās?
Strȳthiō:	fūgērunt, Modeste. mē dēcēpērunt. coēgērunt mē portās omnium cellārum aperīre.
Modestus:	ēheu! quid facere dēbēmus?
Strȳthiō:	nōbīs statim ē carcere fugiendum est; centuriōnem appropinquantem audiō.
Modestus:	ō Strȳthiō! ō, quam īnfēlīx sum!

5

vīvus alive, living

10

amīcī ē carcere quam celerrimē fugiunt.

About the language 2: more about the imperfect and pluperfect subjunctive

1 In Stages 24 and 25 you have met the 3rd person singular and plural ('he', 'she', 'it' and 'they') of the imperfect and pluperfect subjunctive. For example:

> nēmō sciēbat ubi Britannī **latērent**.
> *Nobody knew where the Britons were lying hidden.*

> centuriō, cum hoc **audīvisset**, saeviēbat.
> *When the centurion had heard this, he was furious.*

2 Now study the forms of the 1st person ('I', 'we') and the 2nd person ('you') of the imperfect and pluperfect subjunctive.

SINGULAR	IMPERFECT	PLUPERFECT
1st person	portārem	portāvissem
2nd person	portārēs	portāvissēs
3rd person	portāret	portāvisset

PLURAL		
1st person	portārēmus	portāvissēmus
2nd person	portārētis	portāvissētis
3rd person	portārent	portāvissent

3 Translate the following examples:

a custōdēs nōs rogāvērunt cūr clāmārēmus.
b nesciēbam quō fūgissēs.
c cum in Britanniā mīlitārem, oppidum Aquās Sūlis saepe vīsitāvī.
d cum cēnam tuam cōnsūmerēs, centuriō tē quaerēbat.
e rēx nōbīs explicāvit quō modō vītam suam servāvissētis.
f cum nōmina recitāvissem, hospitēs ad rēgem dūxī.
g amīcus meus cognōscere voluit ubi habitārētis.
h puella nōs rogāvit cūr rem tam difficilem suscēpissēmus.

In each sentence state whether the subjunctive is 1st or 2nd person singular or plural and whether it is imperfect or pluperfect.

Word patterns: male and female

1   Study the following nouns:

        dominus, leaena, dea, domina, fīlia, captīvus, fīlius, captīva, leō, deus.

    Organise these nouns in pairs and write them out in two columns headed *male* and *female*.

2   Add the following nouns to your columns. Some meanings are given to help you.

    saltātrīx (*dancing girl*), vēnātor (*hunter*), avus (*grandfather*), vēnātrīx, victor, avia, victrīx, ursus (*bear*), lupa (*she-wolf*), lupus, ursa, saltātor.

3   Which endings usually indicate the masculine and feminine forms of a Latin noun?

Practising the language

1   This exercise is based on the story **Modestus custōs** on p.75. Read the story again. Complete each of the sentences below with one of the following groups of words. Then translate the sentence. Use each group of words once only.

        cum Modestus extrā cellam haesitāret
        cum Modestus ad culīnam abiisset
        cum carcerem intrāvissent
        cum arānea in nāsum dēcidisset
        cum lucernam tulisset
        cum Modestus vehementer clāmāret

a   Modestus et Strȳthiō, ..., cellās captīvōrum īnspiciēbant.
b   . . . ., Strȳthiō eum rogāvit cūr timēret.
c   Strȳthiō, ..., Modestō trādidit.
d   . . . ., Vercobrix graviter dormiēbat.
e   . . . ., Modestus fūgit perterritus.
f   . . . ., Strȳthiō in carcere mānsit.

2 Complete each sentence with the correct participle from the list below. Then translate the sentence.

   missōs, līberātī, territa, regressam, tenentēs, passus

   a captīvī, ē cellīs subitō . . . ., ad portam carceris ruērunt.
   b Britannī, hastās in manibus . . . ., castra oppugnāvērunt.
   c ancilla, ā dominō īrātō . . . ., respondēre nōn audēbat.
   d Cogidubnus, tot iniūriās . . . ., Rōmānōs vehementer vituperāvit.
   e māter puellam, ē tabernā tandem . . . ., pūnīvit.
   f centuriō mīlitēs, ex Ītaliā nūper ab Imperātōre . . . ., īnspexit.

3 Translate each English sentence into Latin by selecting correctly from the list of Latin words.

   a *The kind citizens had provided help.*
   | cīvis | benignī | auxilium | praebuērunt |
   | cīvēs | benignōs | auxiliī | praebuerant |

   b *They arrested the soldier in the kitchen of an inn.*
   | mīlitem | per culīnam | tabernae | comprehendunt |
   | mīlitis | in culīnā | tabernārum | comprehendērunt |

   c *Master! Read this letter!*
   | domine | haec | epistula | lege |
   | dominus | hanc | epistulam | legis |

   d *The words of the soothsayer frightened him.*
   | verbum | haruspicis | eum | terruit |
   | verba | haruspicī | eōs | terruērunt |

   e *The old men departed, praising the brave messenger.*
   | senēs | discēdunt | fortem | nūntium | laudāns |
   | senum | discessērunt | fortī | nūntiōs | laudantēs |

   f *How can we avoid the punishments of the gods?*
   | quō modō | poenae | deōrum | vītantēs | possumus |
   | quis | poenās | deīs | vītāre | poterāmus |

Building camps and bridges were among the skills required of the army. In this picture, auxiliary soldiers (see page 87) stand guard while soldiers from the legions do engineering work.

The legionary soldier

The soldiers who served in the legions formed the élite of the Roman army. They were all Roman citizens and full-time professionals who had signed on for twenty-five years. They were highly trained in the skills of infantry warfare and were often specialists in other fields as well. In fact a Roman legion, consisting normally of about 5,000 foot soldiers, was a miniature army in itself, capable of constructing forts and camps, manufacturing its weapons and equipment and building roads. On its staff were engineers, architects, carpenters, smiths, doctors, medical orderlies, clerks and accountants.

Recruitment

When he joined the army a new recruit would first be interviewed to ensure that he had the proper legal status, i.e. that he was a Roman citizen; he was also given a medical examination. Vegetius, who wrote a military manual, laid down guidelines for choosing recruits:

A young soldier should have alert eyes and should hold his head upright. The recruit should be broad-chested with powerful shoulders and brawny arms. His fingers should be long rather than short. He should not be pot-bellied or have a fat bottom. His calves and feet should not be flabby: instead they should be made entirely of tough sinew.

In choosing or rejecting recruits, it is important to find out what trade they have been following. Fishermen, birdcatchers, sweet-makers, weavers and all those who do the kind of jobs that women normally do should be kept away from the army. On the other hand, smiths, carpenters, butchers and hunters of deer and wild boar are the most suitable kind of recruit. The whole well-being of the Roman state depends on the kind of recruits you choose; so you must choose men who are outstanding not only in body but also in mind.

Training

After being accepted and sworn in, the new recruit was sent to his unit to begin training. This was thorough, systematic and physically hard. First the young soldier had to learn to march at the regulation pace for distances of up to 24 Roman miles (about 22 statute miles or 35 km). Physical fitness was further developed by running, jumping, swimming and carrying heavy packs. Next came weapon training, starting with a wooden practice-sword and wicker shield. Soldiers learned to handle their shields correctly and to attack dummy targets with the point of their swords. Vegetius again:

> They are also taught not to cut with their swords but to thrust. The Romans find it so easy to beat people who use their swords to cut rather than thrust that they laugh in their faces. For a cutting stroke, even when made with full force, rarely kills. The vital organs are protected by the armour as well as by the bones of the body. On the other hand, a stab even two inches deep is usually fatal.

A centurion, a legionary and the aquilifer (eagle-bearer) of the legion.

The second phase of weapon training was to learn to throw the javelin (**pīlum**). This had a wooden shaft 1.5 metres long and a pointed iron head of 0.6 metres. The head was cleverly constructed. The first 25 centimetres were finely tempered to give it penetrating power, but the rest was left untempered so that it was fairly soft and liable to bend. Thus when the javelin was hurled at an enemy, from a distance of 23–28 metres, its point penetrated and stuck into his shield, while the neck of the metal head bent and the shaft hung down. This not only made the javelin unusable, so that it could not be thrown back, but also made the encumbered shield so difficult to manage that the enemy might have to abandon it altogether.

When he could handle his weapons competently and was physically fit, the soldier was ready to leave the barracks for training in the open countryside. This began with route marches on which he carried not only his body armour and weapons but also several days' ration of food, together with equipment for making an overnight camp, such as a saw, an axe and also a basket for moving earth, as shown in the picture on the right. Much importance was attached to the proper construction of the camp at the end of the day's march, and the young soldier was given careful instruction and practice. Several practice camps and forts have been found in Britain. For example, at Cawthorn in Yorkshire the soldiers under training did rather more than just dig ditches and ramparts; they also constructed platforms for catapults (**ballistae**) and even built camp ovens.

Soldiers marching with their kit slung from a stake.

Work

The fully trained legionary did not spend all or even much of his time on active service. Most of it was spent on peacetime duties, such as building or roadmaking and he was given free time and leave. During the first century AD at least, he had good prospects of surviving till his discharge. He was generally stationed in a large legionary fortress somewhere near the frontiers of the empire in places such as Deva (Chester), Eboracum (York), Bonna (Bonn) and Vindobona (Vienna) which were key points in the Roman defences against the barbarians.

Many of the daily duties were the same wherever he was stationed. A duty roster, written on papyrus, has come down to us and lists the names of thirty-six soldiers, all members of the same century in one of the legions stationed in Egypt. It covers the first ten days in October possibly in the year AD 87. For example, C. Julius Valens was to spend October 3rd and 4th in the limestone quarries, October 5th and 6th in the armoury and October 7th in the bath house, probably stoking the furnace.

A rough carving of a legionary soldier stationed at Bonna, and employed on quarrying duties. He can be recognised as a soldier by his military belt (cingulum).

The Ermine Street Guard demonstrating legionaries'
training. Clockwise from top left: replica of a sword found
in London; swords were used to thrust, not slash; the pilum;
practice with wooden swords and wicker shields.

Pay

In both war and peacetime the soldier received the same rate of pay. In the first century AD, up to the time of the Emperor Domitian (AD 81–96), this amounted to 225 denarii per annum; Domitian improved the rate to 300 denarii. These amounts were gross pay; before any money was handed to the soldier certain deductions were made. Surprising though it may seem, he was obliged to pay for his food, clothing and equipment. He would also leave some money in the military savings bank. What he actually received in cash may have been only a quarter or a fifth of his gross pay. Whether he felt badly treated is difficult to say. Certainly we know of cases of discontent and – very occasionally – mutiny, but pay and conditions of service were apparently not bad enough to discourage recruits. The soldier could look forward to some promotion and eventually an honourable discharge with a lump sum of 3,000 denarii or an allocation of land.

Promotion

If a soldier was promoted his life began to change in several ways. He was paid more and he was exempted from many of the duties performed by the ordinary soldier. Each century was commanded by a centurion who was assisted by an **optiō**. There was also in each century a standard-bearer (**signifer**), a **tesserārius** who organised the guards and distributed the passwords, and one or two clerks.

The centurions, who were roughly equivalent to warrant officers in a modern army, were the backbone of the legion. Most of them had long experience in the army and had risen from the ranks because of their courage and ability. There were sixty of them, each responsible for the training and discipline of a century, and their importance was reflected in their pay, which was probably about 1,500 denarii per annum. The senior centurion of the legion (**prīmus pīlus**) was a highly respected figure; he was at least fifty years old and had worked his way up through the various grades of centurion. He held office for one year, then received a large payment and was allowed to retire; or he might go on still further to become commander of the camp (**praefectus castrōrum**).

Centurion in the Ermine Street Guard, wearing his helmet with transverse plume and decorations, and leaning on his vine-wood staff (vītis).

Diagram of a legion.

 praefectus castrorum

 legatus

 tribunus laticlavius

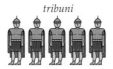 *tribuni*

 aquilifer

FIRST COHORT: 5 centuries = *c.* 800 men

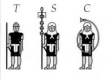

T *S* *C*

centurio primipilus *optio* *centurio*

| *about 160 men* | *about 160 men* | *about 160 men* | *about 160 men* | *about 160 men* |

SECOND TO TENTH COHORTS: 9 cohorts, 6 centuries each, total *c.* 4320 men

T *S* *C*

| *about 80 men* | *about 80 men* | *about 80 men* | *about 80 men* | *about 80 men* | *about 80 men* |

HORSEMEN: about 120

Key

T = tesserarius
S = signifer
C = cornicen (horn-player)
Each **cohort** had one of each of these.
Each **century** had a centurion and an optio.

The auxiliaries

The heavily armed legionaries formed the best trained fighting force in the Roman army, but they needed to be supplemented by large numbers of cavalry and other specialised troops. These were provided by men from different parts of the empire who had developed particular skills, for example, archers from Arabia and slingers from Majorca and Minorca. The most important and prestigious were the cavalry, who were regularly used in battle to support the infantry. They were usually positioned on each side of the legionaries from where they could protect the centre, launch attacks themselves or pursue defeated enemy forces.

Auxiliaries were paid less than legionary soldiers, but when they completed their service those who were not already Roman citizens were granted citizenship. This was another way of making people in the provinces feel loyalty to Roman rule.

Vocabulary checklist 25

accidō, accidere, accidī	*happen*
aliquis	*someone*
aperiō, aperīre, aperuī, apertus	*open*
autem	*but*
castra, castrōrum	*camp*
cōgō, cōgere, coēgī, coāctus	*force, compel*
cōnfīdō, cōnfīdere	*trust*
dignitās, dignitātis	*importance, prestige*
explicō, explicāre, explicāvī, explicātus	*explain*
extrā	*outside*
lateō, latēre, latuī	*lie hidden*
nescio, nescīre, nescīvī	*not know*
nōmen, nōminis	*name*
perītus, perīta, perītum	*skilful*
poena, poenae	*punishment*
poenās dare	*pay the penalty, be punished*
rūrsus	*again*
scelestus, scelesta, scelestum	*wicked*
suāvis, suāve	*sweet*
testis, testis	*witness*

A Roman soldier's dagger.

AGRICOLA

STAGE 26

adventus Agricolae

mīlitēs legiōnis secundae, quī Dēvae in castrīs erant, diū et
strēnuē labōrābant. nam Gāius Iūlius Sīlānus, lēgātus legiōnis,
adventum Agricolae exspectābat. mīlitēs, ā centuriōnibus iussī,
multa et varia faciēbant. aliī arma poliēbant; aliī aedificia
pūrgābant; aliī plaustra reficiēbant.   5

    mīlitēs, ignārī adventūs Agricolae, rem graviter ferēbant. trēs
continuōs diēs labōrāvērunt; quārtō diē Sīlānus adventum
Agricolae nūntiāvit. mīlitēs, cum hoc audīvissent, maximē
gaudēbant quod Agricolam dīligēbant.

    tertiā hōrā Sīlānus mīlitēs in ōrdinēs longōs īnstrūxit, ut   10
Agricolam salūtārent. mīlitēs, cum Agricolam castra intrantem
vīdissent, magnum clāmōrem sustulērunt:

    'iō, Agricola! iō, iō, Agricola!'

    Agricola ad tribūnal prōcessit ut pauca dīceret. omnēs statim
tacuērunt ut Agricolam audīrent.   15

    'gaudeō', inquit, 'quod hodiē vōs rūrsus videō. nūllam
legiōnem fidēliōrem habeō, nūllam fortiōrem. disciplīnam
studiumque vestrum valdē laudō.'

    mīlitēs ita hortātus, per ōrdinēs prōcessit ut eōs īnspiceret.
deinde prīncipia intrāvit ut colloquium cum Sīlānō habēret.   20

adventus *arrival*
legiōnis: legiō *legion*
Dēvae *at Chester*
strēnuē *hard, energetically*
aliī ... aliī ... aliī *some ...*
   others ... others
arma *arms, weapons*
poliēbant: polīre *polish*
pūrgābant: pūrgāre *clean*
trēs ... diēs *for three days*
continuōs: continuus
   continuous, on end
quārtō diē *on the fourth day*
gaudēbant: gaudēre *be*
   pleased, rejoice
tertiā hōrā *at the third hour*
iō! *hurray!*
tribūnal *platform*
disciplīnam: disciplīna
   discipline, orderliness
studium *enthusiasm, keenness*
vestrum: vester *your*
hortātus *having encouraged*
prīncipia *headquarters*

How we know about Agricola

The two inscriptions below both contain the name of Gnaeus
Julius Agricola. The first is on a lead water-pipe found at Chester.

With the abbreviated words written out, this reads:

> imperatore Vespasiano VIIII Tito imperatore VII consulibus
> Cnaeo Iulio Agricola legato Augusti propraetore.

This shows that the pipe was made in AD 79, when Vespasian and
Titus were consuls and Agricola was governor of Britain.
   The inscription drawn below was found in the forum of
Verulamium (modern St Albans). Only fragments have survived,
giving us the letters in red. But it is possible to guess at the rest of
the first five lines because they contain only the names and titles
of the emperor Titus, his brother and successor Domitian, and
Agricola. There is not enough left to reconstruct the last line.

```
IMP·TITVS·CAESAR·DIVI·VESPASIANI·F·VESPASIANVS·AVG
P·M·TR·PVIIII·IMPXV·COSVIIDESIG·VIIII·CENSOR·PATER·PATRIAE
ET·CAESAR·DIVI·VESPASIANI·F·DOMITIANVS·COS·VI·DESIG·VII
PRINCEPS·IVVENTVTIS·COLLEGIORVM·OMNIVM·SACERDOS
         CN·IVLIO·AGRICOLA·LEG·AVG·PRO·PR
              VE              NATA
```

   These inscriptions might have been virtually all that we knew
about the man if his life-story had not been written by his son-in-
law, the historian Tacitus.

in prīncipiīs

When you have read this story, answer the questions at the end.

Salvius ipse paulō prius ad castra advēnerat. iam in legiōnis
secundae prīncipiīs sedēbat, Agricolam anxius exspectāns.
sollicitus erat quod in epistulā, quam ad Agricolam mīserat,
multa falsa scrīpserat. in prīmīs Cogidubnum sēditiōnis
accūsāverat. in animō volvēbat num Agricola sibi crēditūrus   5
esset. Belimicum sēcum dūxerat ut testis esset.

    subitō Salvius, Agricolam intrantem cōnspicātus, ad eum
festīnāvit ut salūtāret. deinde commemorāvit ea quae in epistulā
scrīpserat. Agricola, cum haec audīvisset, diū tacuit. dēnique
maximē commōtus,   10
    'quanta perfidia!' inquit. 'quanta īnsānia! id quod mihi
patefēcistī, vix intellegere possum. ego et Cogidubnus diū amīcī
sumus. īnsānīvit rēx. īnsānīvērunt prīncipēs Rēgnēnsium.
numquam barbarīs crēdere dēbēmus; semper nōs prōdunt.'
    haec locūtus, ad Sīlānum, lēgātum legiōnis, sē vertit.   15
    'Sīlāne', inquit, 'necesse est nōbīs rēgem prīncipēsque
Rēgnēnsium quam celerrimē opprimere. tibi statim cum duābus
cohortibus proficīscendum est.'
    Sīlānus, ē prīncipiīs ēgressus, centuriōnibus mandāta dedit.
eōs iussit cohortēs parāre. intereā Agricola plūra dē rēgis   20
perfidiā rogāre coepit. Salvius eī respondit,
    'ecce Belimicus, vir ingeniī optimī summaeque fideī, quem
iste Cogidubnus corrumpere temptābat. Belimicus autem, quī
blanditiās rēgis spernēbat, omnia mihi patefēcit.'
    'id quod Salvius dīxit vērum est', inquit Belimicus. 'rēx   25
Rōmānōs ōdit. Rōmānōs ē Britanniā expellere tōtamque īnsulam
occupāre cupit. nāvēs igitur comparat. mīlitēs exercet. etiam
bēstiās saevās colligit. nūper bēstiam in mē impulit ut mē
interficeret.'
    Agricola tamen hīs verbīs diffīsus, Salvium dīligentius   30
rogāvit quae indicia sēditiōnis vīdisset. cognōscere voluit quot
essent armātī, num Britannī cīvēs Rōmānōs interfēcissent, quās
urbēs dēlēvissent.
    subitō magnum clāmōrem omnēs audīvērunt. per iānuam
prīncipiōrum perrūpit homō squālidus. ad Agricolam praeceps   35
cucurrit genibusque eius haesit.
    'cīvis Rōmānus sum', inquit. 'Quīntum Caecilium Iūcundum
mē vocant. ego multās iniūriās passus hūc tandem advēnī. hoc
ūnum dīcere volō. Cogidubnus est innocēns.'
    haec locūtus humī prōcubuit exanimātus.   40

paulō prius *a little earlier*

falsa: falsum *lie, untruth*
in prīmīs *in particular*
sēditiōnis: sēditiō *rebellion*
in animō volvēbat: in animō
   volvere *wonder, turn over in*
   the mind
num *whether*
crēditūrus *going to believe*
īnsānia *madness, insanity*

prōdunt: prōdere *betray*

opprimere *crush*
tibi … proficīscendum est
   you must set out
cohortibus: cohors *cohort*

corrumpere *corrupt*
blanditiās: blanditiae
   flatteries
spernēbat: spernere *despise,*
   reject
colligit: colligere *collect*

diffīsus *having distrusted*
indicia: indicium *sign,*
   evidence
quot *how many*

perrūpit: perrumpere *burst*
   through, burst in
squālidus *covered in dirt,*
   filthy

Questions

1   Why was Salvius in the headquarters?   1
2   Why is he described as **sollicitus** (lines 3–4)?   2
3   What particular accusation had he made?   1
4   Why had he brought Belimicus with him?   1
5   **Agricola ... diū tacuit** (line 9). Why do you think Agricola did not
     reply immediately?   1
6   In lines 11–14 did Agricola end by believing or disbelieving Salvius?
     Give a reason for your answer.   1
7   What did Agricola tell Silanus they must do? What order was
     Silanus given (lines 16–18)?   2 + 1
8   In the meantime what did Agricola try to find out?   1
9   How did Salvius describe Belimicus' character? According to
     Salvius, how had Belimicus helped him (lines 22–4)?   2 + 2
10 From Belimicus' information in lines 25–9 find one thing that
     Agricola might have believed and one thing about which he
     might have had doubts.   2
11 In lines 31–3 Agricola asked Salvius for evidence of the rebellion.
     What three things did he want to find out?   3
12 Why do you think Salvius would have found the questions difficult
     to answer?   1
13 What caused the uproar (lines 34–5)?   1
14 What two things did the **homō squālidus** do (lines 35–6)?   2
15 **haec locūtus humī prōcubuit exanimātus** (line 40). Which three
     Latin words in his speech explain why he suddenly collapsed?   1

                                                                ___
                                                       TOTAL   **25**

About the language 1: purpose clauses

1   Study the following examples:

> mīlitēs ad prīncipia convēnērunt **ut Agricolam audīrent**.
> *The soldiers gathered at the headquarters **in order that they might hear Agricola**.*

> per tōtam noctem labōrābat medicus **ut vulnera mīlitum sānāret**.
> *The doctor worked all night **in order that he might treat the soldiers' wounds**.*

The groups of words in **bold type** are known as purpose clauses, because they indicate the purpose for which an action was done. The verb in a purpose clause in Latin is always subjunctive.

2   Further examples:

   a omnēs cīvēs ad silvam contendērunt ut leōnem mortuum spectārent.
   b dominus stilum et cērās poposcit ut epistulam scrīberet.
   c dēnique ego ad patrem rediī ut rem explicārem.
   d pugiōnem rapuī ut captīvum interficerem.
   e equōs celeriter cōnscendimus ut ex oppidō fugerēmus.
   f vīllam intrāvistī ut pecūniam nostram caperēs.

3   Instead of translating **ut** and the subjunctive as *in order that I (you, s/he, etc.) might ...*, it is often possible to use a simpler form of words:

> mīlitēs ad prīncipia convēnērunt ut Agricolam audīrent.
> *The soldiers gathered at the headquarters in order to hear Agricola.*

Or, simpler still:
> *The soldiers gathered at the headquarters to hear Agricola.*

tribūnus

tribūnus *tribune (high-ranking officer)*

Agricola, ubi hoc vīdit, custōdēs iussit Quīntum auferre medicumque arcessere. tum ad tribūnum mīlitum, quī adstābat, sē vertit.

adstābat: adstāre *stand by*

'mī Rūfe', inquit, 'prūdentissimus es omnium tribūnōrum quōs habeō. tē iubeō hunc hominem summā cum cūrā interrogāre.'   5

prūdentissimus: prūdēns *shrewd, intelligent*

Salvius, cum Rūfus exiisset, valdē commōtus, 'omnia explicāre possum', inquit. 'nōtus est mihi hic homō. nūper in vīllā mē vīsitāvit, quamquam nōn invītāveram. trēs mēnsēs apud mē mānsit, opēs meās dēvorāns. duōs tripodas argenteōs habēbam, quōs abstulit ut Cogidubnō daret. sed eum nōn accūsāvī, quod hospes erat. ubi tamen Aquās Sūlis mēcum advēnit, facinus scelestum committere temptāvit. venēnum parāvit ut Memorem, haruspicem Rōmānum, necāret. postquam rem nōn effēcit, mē ipsum accūsāvit. nōlī eī crēdere. multō perfidior est quam Britannī.'   15

10

opēs *money, wealth*
dēvorāns: dēvorāre *devour, eat up*

multō perfidior *much more treacherous*

haec cum audīvisset, Agricola respondit,
'sī haec fēcit, eī moriendum est.'
mox revēnit Rūfus valdē attonitus.

sī *if*

'Quīntus Caecilius', inquit, 'est iuvenis summae fideī. patrem meum, quem Alexandrīae relīquī, bene nōverat. hoc prō certō habeō quod Quīntus hanc epistulam mihi ostendit, ā patre ipsō scrīptam.'   20

Alexandrīae *at Alexandria*
prō certō habeō: prō certō habēre *know for certain*

Agricola statim Quīntum ad sē vocāvit, cēterōsque dīmīsit. Salvius, Quīntum dētestātus, anxius exiit. Agricola cum Quīntō colloquium trēs hōrās habēbat.   25

dētestātus *having cursed*

king midas has ass's ears

Chester was founded at the highest point on the River Dee that sea-going ships could reach. Part of the Roman quayside can be seen today.

About the language 2: gerundives

1 From Stage 14 onwards you have met sentences of this kind:

> necesse est mihi ad castra contendere.   necesse est vōbīs labōrāre.
> *I must hurry to the camp.*   *You must work.*

2 You have now met another way of expressing the same idea:

> necesse est nōbīs currere.   necesse est eī revenīre.
> nōbīs **currendum** est.   eī **reveniendum** est.
> *We must run.*   *He must come back.*

The word in **bold type** is known as the gerundive

3 Further examples:

   a mihi fugiendum est.
   b nōbīs ambulandum est.
   c tibi hīc manendum est.
   d servīs dīligenter labōrandum est.
   e omnibus cīvibus tacendum est quod sacerdōtēs appropinquant.
   f sī Imperātōrem vidēre volunt, eīs festīnandum est.

contentiō

Agricola, cum Quīntum audīvisset, Salvium furēns arcessīvit.
quī, simulatque intrāvit, aliquid dīcere coepit. Agricola tamen,
cum silentium iussisset, Salvium vehementer accūsāvit.

'dī immortālēs! Cogidubnus est innocēns, tū perfidus. cūr
tam īnsānus eram ut tibi crēderem? simulatque ad hanc   5
prōvinciam vēnistī, amīcī mē dē calliditāte tuā monuērunt. nunc
rēs ipsa mē docuit. num Imperātor Domitiānus hanc tantam
perfidiam ferre potest? ego sānē nōn possum. in hāc prōvinciā
summam potestātem habeō. iubeō tē hās inimīcitiās dēpōnere.   **inimīcitiās: inimīcitia** *feud,*
iubeō tē ad Cogidubnī aulam īre, veniamque ab eō petere.   10   *quarrel*
praetereā Imperātōrī ipsī rem explicāre dēbēs.'

haec ubi dīxit Agricola, Salvius respondit īrātus,
'quam caecus es! quam longē errās! tū ipse Imperātōrī id   **caecus** *blind*
quod in Britanniā facis explicāre dēbēs. tū enim in ultimīs
Britanniae partibus bellum geris et victōriās inānēs ē Calēdoniā   15 **victōriās: victōria** *victory*
refers; sed Imperātor pecūniam opēsque accipere cupit. itaque   **inānēs: inānis** *empty,*
rēgnum Cogidubnī occupāre cōnstituit; Calēdoniam nōn cūrat.   *meaningless*
tū sānē hoc nescīs. in magnō perīculō es, quod cōnsilium meum   **Calēdoniā: Calēdonia**
spernis. nōn sōlum mihi sed Imperātōrī ipsī obstās.'   *Scotland*

cum hanc contentiōnem inter sē habērent, subitō nūntius   20   **cōnstituit: cōnstituere** *decide*
prīncipia ingressus exclāmāvit,
'mortuus est Cogidubnus!'

Word patterns: verbs and nouns

1 Some verbs and nouns are closely connected. For example:

Imperātor Cogidubnum **honōrāre** volēbat.
The Emperor wanted to honour Cogidubnus.

magnōs **honōrēs** ab Imperātōre accēpit.
He received great honours from the Emperor.

terra valdē **tremere** coepit.
The earth began to shake violently.

cīvēs magnum **tremōrem** sēnsērunt.
The citizens felt a great shaking.

2 Further examples:

verbs		nouns	
amāre	*to love*	amor	*love*
clāmāre	*to shout*	clāmor	*a shout, shouting*
terrēre	*to terrify*	terror	*terror*

3 Now complete the table below:

timēre	*to fear*	timor	....
dolēre	(1) *to hurt, to be in pain*	dolor	(1) ....
dolēre	(2) *to grieve*	dolor	(2) ....
favēre	....	favor	*favour*
furere	....	furor	*rage*
labōrāre	....	....	....

Practising the language

1 Complete each sentence with the correct form of the noun. Then translate the sentence.

    a Agricola, ubi verba . . . . audīvit, Salvium arcessīvit. (Quīntum, Quīntī, Quīntō)

    b omnēs hospitēs . . . . saltātrīcis laudāvērunt. (artem, artis, artī)

    c iter nostrum difficile erat, quod tot cīvēs . . . . complēbant. (viās, viārum, viīs)

    d prō prīncipiīs stābat magna turba . . . . (mīlitēs, mīlitum, mīlitibus)

    e lēgātus, postquam mandāta . . . . dedit, legiōnem ad montem proximum dūxit. (centuriōnēs, centuriōnum, centuriōnibus)

    f iūdex, quī . . . . nōn crēdēbat, īrātissimus erat. (puerōs, puerōrum, puerīs)

2 Complete each sentence with the right form of the subjunctive. Then translate the sentence.

    a cum Sīlānus legiōnem . . . ., Agricola ē prīncipiīs prōcessit. (īnstrūxisset, īnstrūxissent)

    b mīlitēs in flūmen dēsiluērunt ut hostēs . . . . (vītāret, vītārent)

    c senātor scīre voluit num pater meus Imperātōrī . . . . (fāvisset, fāvissent)

    d cum senex . . . ., fūrēs per fenestram tacitē intrāvērunt. (dormīret, dormīrent)

    e nōs, cum in Britanniā . . . ., barbarōs saepe vīcimus. (essem, essēmus)

    f intellegere nōn poteram cūr cīvēs istum hominem . . . . (laudāvisset, laudāvissent)

    g latrōnem interfēcī ut īnfantem . . . . (servārem, servārēmus)

    h māter tua mē rogāvit quid in tabernā . . . . (fēcissēs, fēcissētis)

3 Complete each sentence with the correct word from the list below. Then translate the sentence.

       epistulam, audīvisset, ēgressus, invēnērunt, equīs, captī

    a Salvius, ē prīncipiīs . . . ., Belimicum quaesīvit.

    b Agricola, cum haec verba . . . ., ad Rūfum sē vertit.

    c dominus . . . . ē manibus servī furēns rapuit.

    d custōdēs nūntium sub aquā iacentem . . . .

    e quattuor Britannī, in pugnā . . . ., vītam dūrissimam in carcere agēbant.

    f aliī mīlitēs . . . . aquam dabant, aliī frūmentum in horrea īnferēbant.

The senior officers in the Roman army

The officer commanding a legion was called a **lēgātus**. He was a member of the Senate in Rome and usually in his middle thirties. He was assisted by six military tribunes. Of these, one was usually a young man of noble birth, serving his military apprenticeship before starting a political career. After holding civilian posts in Rome or one of the provinces, he might be appointed as legatus and spend three or four years commanding his legion. He would then usually resume his civilian career.

The other five tribunes were members of a slightly lower social class and they too would be in their thirties. They were generally able, wealthy and educated men, often aiming at important posts in the imperial administration. Some of them returned to the army to command auxiliary cavalry units.

The senior officers usually spent only short periods in the army, unlike the centurions and the legionaries who served for the whole of their working lives. They had therefore to rely heavily on the expertise and experience of the centurions for advice. Because the army was highly trained and well organised, the appointment of relatively inexperienced officers rarely affected the success of its operations.

Some officers like Agricola proved themselves to be extremely competent and were promoted to become governors of provinces like Britain where military skill and powers of leadership were required.

The god Mars, wearing the helmet, breastplate and greaves of a senior officer.

Agricola, governor of Britain

Agricola was born in AD 40 in the Roman colony of Forum Iulii (modern Fréjus) in south-east Gaul. His father had been made a senator by the Emperor Tiberius, but later fell foul of the Emperor Gaius Caligula and was executed shortly after Agricola was born.

Agricola went to school at Massilia (Marseille), which was the cultural and educational centre of southern Gaul. He followed the normal curriculum for the young sons of upper-class Roman families: public speaking (taught by a **rhētor**) and philosophy. He enjoyed the latter, but Tacitus records his mother's reaction:

'I remember that Agricola often told us that in his youth he was more enthusiastic about philosophy than a Roman and a senator was expected to be, and his mother thought it wise to restrain such a passionate interest.'

At the age of eighteen, Agricola served in the Roman army in Britain with the rank of **tribūnus**. He used this opportunity to become familiar with the province. The soldiers under his command had a similar opportunity to get to know him. Two years later, during the revolt of Boudica in AD 60, he witnessed the grim realities of warfare. Agricola was by now very knowledgeable about the province of Britain and this knowledge was to stand him in good stead during his governorship some eighteen years later.

Back in Rome, he continued his political career. In AD 70, he returned to Britain to take command of the Twentieth Legion which was stationed at Viroconium (Wroxeter) and had become undisciplined and troublesome. His success in handling this difficult task was rewarded by promotion to the governorship of Aquitania in Gaul. He then became consul and in AD 78 returned to Britain for a third time, as governor of the province. The political experience and military skill which he had acquired by then equipped him to face an exciting and demanding situation.

An antefix (a kind of roof tile) made by the Twentieth Legion. The boar was their badge.

Agricola fought the fierce tribes of Scotland. This boar's head is part of one of their war trumpets.

Agricola rose to the challenge in many different ways. He completed the conquest of Wales and then fought a series of successful campaigns in Scotland, culminating in a great victory at Mons Graupius in the north of the Grampian mountains. He extended the network of roads and forts across northern Britain and established the legionary fortress at Chester.

In addition to his military exploits Agricola carried out an extensive programme of romanisation. His biographer Tacitus tells us that he 'encouraged individuals and helped communities to build temples, fora and houses in the Roman style'. As we have seen, the inscription from the new forum at Verulamium records his name.

Tacitus also tells us of his plans to improve the education of the British:

'Agricola arranged for the sons of British chiefs to receive a broad education. He made it clear that he preferred the natural abilities of the British to the skill and training of the Gauls. As a result, instead of hating the language of the Romans, they became very keen to learn it.'

Snow lies between the earthworks of Chew Green, one of the camps first built by Agricola on his way to conquer the Caledonians of Scotland. The photograph is looking south; the modern road in the distance follows the line of the Roman Dere Street.

Agricola was governor of Britain for seven years, longer than any other Roman governor, and during this time the area under direct Roman control was nearly doubled. When he returned to Rome, Agricola was given the honours due to a successful general, including a splendid statue. This was the end of his career; any hopes he may have had of a further governorship were not fulfilled and he may have died a disappointed man.

A Roman cavalryman triumphing over Caledonians: a sculpture put up on a later Roman frontier in Scotland, the Antonine Wall.

Vocabulary checklist 26

auferō, auferre, abstulī, ablātus	take away, steal
bellum, bellī	war
bellum gerere	wage war, campaign
commōtus, commōta, commōtum	moved, excited, upset
doceō, docēre, docuī, doctus	teach
falsus, falsa, falsum	false, dishonest
fidēs, fideī	loyalty, trustworthiness
īnstruō, īnstruere, īnstrūxī, īnstrūctus	draw up
lēgātus, lēgātī	commander
legiō, legiōnis	legion
nōtus, nōta, nōtum	known, well-known, famous
num	whether
praebeō, praebēre, praebuī, praebitus	offer, provide
quot?	how many?
referō, referre, rettulī, relātus	bring back, carry
rēgnum, rēgnī	kingdom
saevus, saeva, saevum	savage, cruel
sī	if
ultimus, ultima, ultimum	furthest
ut	that, in order that

A small figure of a teacher reading from a scroll. Agricola encouraged the British to learn Latin.

IN CASTRIS

STAGE 27

1 'fuge mēcum ad horreum!'

Modestus et Strȳthiō sermōnem anxiī
habēbant.
    Modestus Strȳthiōnem monēbat ut ad
horreum sēcum fugeret.

2 'invenīte Modestum Strȳthiōnemque!'

prō prīncipiīs, centuriō mīlitibus mandāta
dabat.   *dative*
    centuriō mīlitibus imperābat ut
Modestum Strȳthiōnemque invenīrent.

3 'castra Rōmāna oppugnāte! horrea
incendite!'

direct
speech   in silvā proximā, Vercobrix ōrātiōnem apud
Britannōs habēbat.
    Vercobrix Britannōs incitābat ut castra
Rōmāna oppugnārent et horrea incenderent.

in horreō

Modestus et Strȳthiō, ē carcere ēgressī, ad horreum fūgērunt. per aditum angustum rēpsērunt et in horreō cēlātī manēbant. centuriō, cum portās cellārum apertās carceremque dēsertum vīdisset, īrātissimus erat. mīlitibus imperāvit ut Modestum et Strȳthiōnem caperent. mīlitēs tamen, quamquam per tōta castra quaerēbant, eōs invenīre nōn poterant. illī duōs diēs mānsērunt cēlātī. tertiō diē Modestus tam miser erat ut rem diūtius ferre nōn posset.

Modestus:	quam īnfēlīx sum! mālim in illō carcere esse potius quam in hōc horreō latēre. ēheu! ubīque frūmentum videō, sed cōnsūmere nōn possum. quālis est haec vīta?
Strȳthiō:	mī Modeste, difficile est nōbīs hīc diūtius manēre. nunc tamen advesperāscit. vīsne mē, ex horreō ēgressum, cibum quaerere? hominibus miserrimīs cibus spem semper affert.
Modestus:	id est cōnsilium optimum. nōbīs cēnandum est. Strȳthiō, ī prīmum ad coquum. eum iubē cēnam splendidam coquere et hūc portāre. deinde quaere Aulum et Pūblicum, amīcōs nostrōs! invītā eōs ad cēnam! iubē Aulum amphoram vīnī ferre, Pūblicum lucernam. tum curre ad vīcum; Nigrīnam quaere! optima est saltātrīcum; mihi saltātrīcēs semper sōlācium afferunt.
Strȳthiō:	quid dīcis? vīsne mē saltātrīcem in castra dūcere?
Modestus:	abī caudex!

Strȳthiō, ut mandāta Modestī efficeret, celeriter discessit. coquō persuāsit ut cēnam splendidam parāret; Aulō et Pūblicō persuāsit ut vīnum lucernamque ferrent; Nigrīnam ōrāvit ut in castra venīret, sed eī persuādēre nōn poterat.

aditum: aditus *opening*
angustum: angustus *narrow*
rēpsērunt: rēpere *crawl*
imperāvit: imperāre *order, command*

mālim *I should prefer*
potius *rather*

advesperāscit: advesperāscere *get dark, become dark*
spem: spēs *hope*
affert: afferre *bring*
prīmum *first*

vīcum: vīcus *town, village*

sōlācium *comfort*

ōrāvit: ōrāre *beg*

5

10

15

20

25

30

Reconstruction of a granary at the Lunt fort, near Coventry.

About the language 1: indirect commands

1   In Book I, you met sentences like this:

    'redīte!'   'pecūniam trāde!'
    'Go back!'   *'Hand over the money'*

In each example, an order or command is being given. These examples are
known as direct commands.

2   In Stage 27, you have met sentences like this:

    lēgātus mīlitibus imperāvit **ut redīrent**.
    *The commander ordered his soldiers **that they should go back**.*
    Or, in more natural English:
    *The commander ordered his soldiers **to go back**.*

    latrōnēs mercātōrī imperāvērunt **ut pecūniam trāderet**.
    *The robbers ordered the merchant **that he should hand over the money**.*
    Or, in more natural English:
    *The robbers ordered the merchant **to hand over the money**.*

In each of these examples, the command is not being given directly, but is
being *reported* or *referred to*. These examples are known as indirect commands.
The verb in an indirect command in Latin is usually subjunctive.

3   Compare the following examples:

direct commands	indirect commands
'contendite!'	iuvenis amīcīs persuāsit ut contenderent.
'Hurry!'	*The young man persuaded his friends to hurry.*
'dā mihi aquam!'	captīvus custōdem ōrāvit ut aquam sibi daret.
'Give me water!'	*The prisoner begged the guard to give him water.*
'fuge!'	mē monuit ut fugerem.
'Run away!'	*He warned me to run away.*

4   Further examples of direct and indirect commands:

   a   'tacē!'
   b   centuriō mihi imperāvit ut tacērem.
   c   'parcite mihi!'
   d   senex nōs ōrābat ut sibi parcerēmus.
   e   nēmō ancillae persuādēre poterat ut saltāret.
   f   coquus servīs imperāvit ut vīnum in mēnsam pōnerent.
   g   vōs saepe monēbam ut dīligenter labōrārētis.
   h   mīlitēs mercātōrem monuērunt ut ab oppidō celeriter discēderet.

Modestus prōmōtus

prōmōtus: prōmovēre
promote

I

cum Strȳthiō cēnam et amīcōs quaereret, decem Britannī, ā
Vercobrige ductī, castrīs cautē appropinquābant. Vercobrix
enim eīs persuāserat ut castra oppugnārent. Britannī, postquam
custōdēs vītāvērunt, castra intrāvērunt. in manibus facēs   **facēs: fax** *torch*
tenēbant ut horrea incenderent. celeriter ad horrea advēnērunt   5
quod prius cognōverant ubi sita essent.

    Modestus, ignārus adventūs Britannōrum, in horreō sedēbat.   **ignārus** *not knowing, unaware*
adeō ēsuriēbat ut dē vītā paene dēspērāret. per aditum
prōspiciēbat, reditum Strȳthiōnis exspectāns.   **prōspiciēbat: prōspicere** *look*
    'trēs hōrās Strȳthiōnem iam exspectō. quid eī accidit?'   10   *out*
subitō manum hominum per tenebrās cōnspexit.
    'euge! tandem vēnērunt amīcī! heus, amīcī, hūc venīte!'
    Britannī, cum Modestī vōcem audīvissent, erant tam attonitī
ut immōtī stārent. respondēre nōn audēbant. Vercobrix tamen,
quī raucam Modestī vōcem agnōverat, ad comitēs versus,   15   **comitēs: comes** *comrade,*
    'nōlīte timēre', inquit susurrāns. 'nōtus est mihi hic mīles.   *companion*
stultior est quam asinus. nōbīs nocēre nōn potest.'   **versus** *having turned*
    tum Britannī per aditum tacitī rēpsērunt. simulatque
intrāvērunt, Modestus eīs obviam iit, ut salūtāret.   **obviam iit: obviam īre** *meet,*
    'salvēte, amīcī! nunc nōbīs cēnandum ac bibendum est.'   20   *go to meet*
    tum Britannus quīdam, vir ingēns, in Modestum incurrit.   **incurrit: incurrere** *bump into*
    'ō Nigrīna, dēliciae meae!' inquit Modestus. 'tē nōn agnōvī!
quam longī sunt capillī tuī! age! cōnsīde prope mē! dā mihi
ōsculum! quis lucernam habet?'

Vercobrix, cum Modestum lucernam rogantem audīvisset, 25
Britannīs imperāvit ut facēs incenderent. Modestus,
Vercobrigem Britannōsque cōnspicātus, palluit.

'dī immortālēs!' inquit. 'abiit Nigrīna, appāruērunt Britannī!
mihi statim effugiendum est.'

II

*When you have read this part of the story, answer the questions at
the end.*

Vercobrix tamen suīs imperāvit ut Modestum comprehenderent.   **suīs: suī** *his men*
ūnus ē Britannīs Modestō appropinquāvit ut dēligāret. fax,
tamen, quam tenēbat, tunicam Modestī forte incendit.

'ēheu!'ululāvit ille. 'ardeō! mē dēvorant flammae!'

tum ē manibus Britannōrum ēlāpsus fūgit praeceps. simulac   5
per aditum ērūpit, Strȳthiōnī amīcīsque occurrit. amphoram vīnī   **occurrit: occurrere** *meet*
ē manibus Aulī ēripuit et vīnum in tunicam fūdit.   **ēripuit: ēripere** *snatch, tear*

'īnsānit Modestus!' clāmāvit Strȳthiō attonitus.

Modestus tamen, Strȳthiōnis clāmōrum neglegēns,
amphoram in aditum impulit. tum in amphoram innīxus,   *10*   **innīxus** *having leant*
magnōs clāmōrēs sustulit.

'subvenīte! subvenīte! Britannōs cēpī!'   **subvenīte: subvenīre** *help,*
      come to help

tantī erant clāmōrēs Modestī ut tōta castra complērent. statim
manus mīlitum, ā centuriōne ducta, ad horrea contendit ut
causam strepitūs cognōsceret.   *15*   **causam: causa** *reason, cause*
    strepitūs: strepitus *noise, din*

Modestus exsultāns 'īnsidiās Britannīs parāvī', inquit.
'Vercobrix ipse multīs cum Britannīs in horreō inclūsus est.'
breve erat certāmen. tantus erat numerus mīlitum
Rōmānōrum ut Britannōs facile superārent. Rōmānī Britannōs
ex horreō extractōs ad carcerem redūxērunt. tum lēgātus   20
legiōnis ipse Modestum arcessītum laudāvit.
    'Modeste', inquit, 'mīlitem fortiōrem quam tē numquam
anteā vīdī. decōrum est nōbīs praemium tibi dare.'
    Modestus, ā lēgātō ita laudātus, adeō gaudēbat ut vix sē
continēre posset. pecūniam laetus exspectābat.   25
    'carcerī tē praeficiō', inquit lēgātus.

breve: brevis *short, brief*
certāmen *struggle, fight*
redūxērunt: redūcere *lead back*

continēre *contain*
praeficiō: praeficere *put in charge of*

Questions

		Marks
1	What order did Vercobrix give his men?	1
2	Explain how Modestus' tunic caught fire (lines 2–3).	3
3	What had Modestus just done to make Strythio exclaim '**īnsānit Modestus**' (line 8)?	2
4	Pick out and translate the Latin words which show that Modestus took no notice of Strythio.	2
5	What did Modestus do next with the amphora (lines 9–10)?	1
6	What success did he then claim?	1
7	Why did the centurion and the soldiers hasten to the granaries (lines 13–15)?	1
8	**breve erat certāmen** (line 18). Explain why this was so.	2
9	What happened to the Britons?	2
10	How did the **lēgātus** congratulate Modestus (lines 22–3)?	2
11	**decōrum est nōbīs praemium tibi dare** (line 23). What reward did Modestus expect? What reward did he actually get?	2
12	Do you think the reward was a suitable one for Modestus? Give a reason.	1

TOTAL **20**

About the language 2: result clauses

1   Study the following examples:

> tanta erat multitūdō **ut tōtam aulam complēret**.
> *So great was the crowd **that it filled the whole palace.***
>
> iuvenis gladium adeō cupiēbat **ut pecūniam statim trāderet**.
> *The young man wanted the sword so much **that he handed over the**
> **money immediately.***

The groups of words in **bold type** are known as result clauses because they indicate a result. The verb in a result clause in Latin is always subjunctive.

2   Further examples:

   a   tam stultus erat puer ut omnēs eum dērīdērent.
   b   tantus erat clāmor ut nēmō iussa centuriōnum audīret.
   c   Agricola tot mīlitēs ēmīsit ut hostēs fugerent.
   d   patrem adeō timēbam ut domum redīre nōn audērem.
   e   tot servōs habēbās ut eōs numerāre nōn possēs.
   f   ancillae nostrae tam dīligenter labōrābant ut eās saepe laudārēmus.

3   Notice that in the first part of each sentence there is a word that signals that a result clause is coming. For example, study the first sentence in paragraph 1. **tanta**, *so great*, is a signal for the result clause **ut tōtam aulam complēret**. In the last three sentences in paragraph 2 what are the signal words? What do they mean?

Word patterns: adjectives and nouns

1 Study the form and meaning of the following adjectives and nouns:

adjectives		nouns	
longus	*long*	longitūdō	*length*
sollicitus	*worried*	sollicitūdō	*worry, anxiety*
altus	*deep*	altitūdō	*depth*

2 Now complete the table below:

solus	*alone, lonely*	solitūdō	....
magnus	....	magnitūdō	....
lātus	*wide*	....	....
mānsuētus	*tame*	mānsuētūdō	....

3 Give the meaning of the following nouns:

fortitūdō, pulchritūdō, multitūdō

4 How many of the Latin nouns in paragraphs 1–3 can be translated into English by a noun ending in -tude? If you are unsure, use an English dictionary to help you.

5 Notice some slightly different examples:

cupere	*to desire*	cupīdō	*desire*
		Cupīdō	*Cupid, the god of desire*
valēre	*to be well*	valētūdō	*health*
			(1) *good health*
			(2) *bad health*

The imperative of **valēre** has a special meaning which you have met before:

valē   *be well*, i.e. *farewell, goodbye*

Practising the language

1 Translate the following examples:

 a faber, prope iānuam tabernae stāns, pugnam spectābat.
 b Vilbia, ē culīnā ēgressa, sorōrem statim quaesīvit.
 c fūrēs, ad iūdicem ductī, veniam petīvērunt.
 d centuriō, amphoram vīnī optimī adeptus, ad amīcōs celeriter rediit.
 e subitō equōs appropinquantēs audīvimus.
 f puer callidus pecūniam, in terrā cēlātam, invēnit.

 Pick out the participle in each sentence and say whether it is present,
 perfect passive or perfect active. Then write down the noun described by
 each participle.

2 Change the words in **bold type** from singular to plural. Then translate the
 new sentences. Some of the sentences contain neuter nouns and you may
 need to refer to the table of nouns on pages 146–7 and to the Vocabulary.

 a Imperātor **īnsulam** vīsitābat.
 b **nauta** pecūniam **poscēbat**.
 c haec verba **senem** terrēbant.
 d iuvenēs **captīvum** custōdiēbant.
 e fūr **pōculum** īnspiciēbat.
 f **leō** ad pāstōrem **contendēbat**.
 g equī **flūmen** trānsīre nōlēbant.
 h **templum** in forō **erat**.

3 With the help of the table of nouns on pages 146–7, complete the sentences
 of this exercise with the right case of each unfinished noun. Then translate
 the sentence.

 a puella tabernam meam intrāvit. puell… multōs ānulōs ostendī.
 b puerī per viam currēbant. clāmōrēs puer… mē excitāvērunt.
 c Salvius ad aulam rēg… quam celerrimē contendit.
 d servī prope iānuam stābant. serv… pecūniam dedimus.
 e Memor, ubi nōm… tuum audīvit, perterritus erat.
 f in hāc viā sunt duo templ… .
 g mercātor ad fundum meum heri vēnit. frūmentum meum mercātōr…
  vēndidī.
 h magna multitūdō cīv… nōbīs obstābat.
 i barbarī prōvinciam oppugnāvērunt, multāsque urb… dēlēvērunt.
 j iūdex mercātōr…, quī fēminam dēcēperat, pūnīvit.

The legionary fortress

If the legion itself was like a miniature army, the fortress in which it lived when not on campaign could be compared to a fortified town. It covered about 20–25 hectares (50–60 acres), about one third of the area of Pompeii. The design of the fortress was based on a standard pattern, illustrated below.

The chief buildings, grouped in the centre, were the headquarters (**prīncipia**), the living-quarters of the commanding officer (**praetōrium**), the hospital (**valētūdinārium**), and the granaries (**horrea**). Numerous streets and alleys criss-crossed the fortress, but there were three main streets: the **via praetōria** ran from the main gate to the front entrance of the principia; the **via prīncipālis** extended across the whole width of the fortress, making a T-junction with the via praetoria just in front of the principia; the **via quīntāna** passed behind the principia and also extended across the width of the fortress. The fortress was surrounded by a ditch, rampart and battlements, with towers at the corners and at intervals along the sides. Each side had a fortified gateway.

The principia was a large and impressive building at the heart of the fortress. A visitor would first enter a stone-flagged courtyard surrounded on three sides by a colonnade and storerooms. On the far side of the courtyard was a great hall or basilica, where the commander worked with his officers, interviewed important local people and administered military justice. It was a surprisingly large hall and would have looked rather like the interior of a cathedral. The one at Chester, for example, was about 73 metres long; its

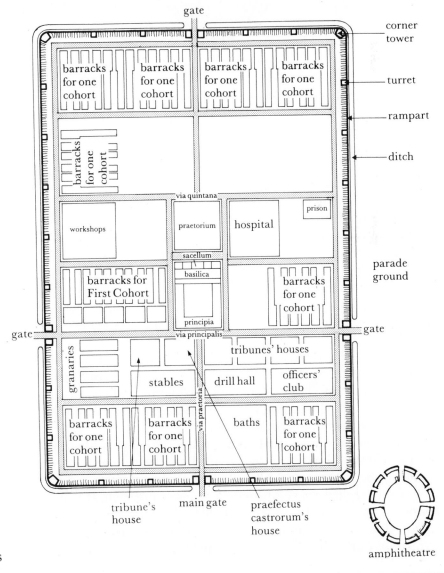

Plan of a legionary fortress (based on Chester).

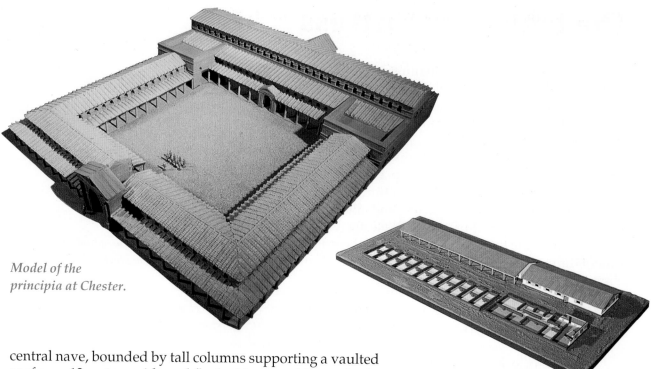

Model of the principia at Chester.

Cutaway model of a pair of barrack blocks.

central nave, bounded by tall columns supporting a vaulted roof, was 12 metres wide and flanked by two aisles each of 6 metres.

In the centre of the far long wall of the basilica and directly facing the main gate was the most sacred place in the fortress, the **sacellum** or chapel. This housed the standard of the legion, the **aquila**, an image of an eagle perched with outspread wings on the top of a pole. It was made of gold and in its talons it clutched a bundle of golden darts that represented the thunderbolts of Jupiter. The aquila represented the spirit of the legion and aroused feelings of intense loyalty and an almost religious respect. To lose it in battle was the worst possible disgrace and misfortune; it rarely happened. The soldier who looked after the aquila and carried it in battle was called the **aquilifer** (eagle-bearer). He was always a soldier of the first cohort.

On either side of the sacellum were the rooms where the clerks kept the payrolls and attended to all the paperwork that was needed to run a large organisation. Close by and usually underground was the legion's strong-room, in which pay and savings were kept under lock and key.

The praetorium was situated by the side of or just behind the principia. It was a luxurious villa in the Italian style and it provided the legatus and his family with those comforts which they would regard as necessary for a civilised life: central heating, a garden and a private suite of baths. The very high standard of the commander's quarters would demonstrate the attractions of Roman civilisation to any local civilian leaders entertained in the praetorium. However, whether this display of wealth made them any happier about the taxes which they had to pay to the Romans is another question.

The valetudinarium or hospital contained many small wards which were designed to ensure peace and quiet for the sick and injured. There was also a large reception hall to accommodate an influx of casualties from the battlefield and a small operating theatre equipped with running water.

The horrea or granaries were skilfully designed to keep grain dry and cool for long periods. In the first century AD, like many other buildings in the fortress, they were built mainly of wood, but from the second century stone was the regular material. A granary was a long and narrow building; the roof had wide overhanging eaves to carry the rain-water away from the walls; and to prevent damp rising from the ground the floor was supported on small piers or low walls which allowed air to circulate freely underneath. There were several of these granaries in a fortress, often arranged side by side in pairs, and they could contain stocks of grain sufficient for at least one year and possibly two.

The barrack blocks, housing 5,000–6,000 men, occupied the largest area. They too were long and narrow; and they were divided into pairs of rooms, each pair providing accommodation for an eight-man section (**contubernium**).

A stone-built granary at Housesteads near Hadrian's Wall.

Along the front of the block ran a colonnaded verandah. Each section cooked for itself on a hearth in the front living-room, which was slightly the smaller of the two rooms, and slept in the larger room at the back. Each block housed a century (80 men). At the end of the block a larger suite of rooms was provided for the centurion, who may have shared it with his optio. The blocks themselves were arranged in pairs facing each other across an alleyway, as in the model on page 116.

The bath house was important both for hygienic reasons and because it provided a social centre for the troops; every fortress and many smaller forts had one. Like the civilian baths, it consisted of a tepidarium, caldarium and frigidarium. Sometimes it was outside the fortress, by a nearby stream or river, sometimes inside.

One other building, always outside, should be mentioned: the amphitheatre. It had the same shape and layout as the civilian amphitheatre and could seat the whole legion. It was used for ceremonial parades, weapon training and displays of tactics, as well as for occasional gladiatorial shows.

Not surprisingly, civilians also tended to gather round military bases. At first they were traders who set up little bars to sell appetising food and drink to supplement the plain rations served in the barracks. Naturally, too, these bars gave soldiers opportunities to meet the local girls. Legally soldiers were not allowed to marry, but the army tolerated unofficial unions. While the father lived in barracks his family grew up just outside; and his sons when they were eighteen or nineteen often followed his profession and enlisted. Many such settlements

A centurion's quarters, based on remains of a wooden barrack block with painted plaster found at Chester.

The remains of the Chester amphitheatre today.

Barrack blocks and the amphitheatre.

(**vīcī**) developed gradually into towns. A few became large, self-governing cities, such as Eboracum (York). Thus the military fortress, which had begun as a means of holding down newly conquered territory, ended by playing an important part in the development of civilian town life.

The Roman fortress – from timber to stone

The Romans first built their fortresses of wood, for speed, and later rebuilt them in stone. The top picture shows a reconstruction of a wooden gate at the Lunt fort, Coventry (seen from the inside). Below is a stone gateway (seen from the outside) rebuilt at Arbeia fortress, South Shields, a supply base.

Vocabulary checklist 27

adeō	*so much, so greatly*
anteā	*before*
appāreō, appārēre, appāruī	*appear*
ardeō, ardēre, arsī	*burn, be on fire*
comes, comitis	*comrade, companion*
gaudeō, gaudēre	*be pleased, rejoice*
ignārus, ignāra, ignārum	*not knowing, unaware*
imperō, imperāre, imperāvī	*order, command*
incendō, incendere, incendī, incēnsus	*burn, set on fire*
īnsidiae, īnsidiārum	*trap, ambush*
iussum, iussī	*instruction, order*
manus, manūs	*hand, band (of men)*
noceō, nocēre, nocuī	*hurt, harm*
praeceps, *gen.* praecipitis	*headlong*
praemium, praemiī	*prize, reward, profit*
proximus, proxima, proximum	*nearest*
quālis, quāle	*what sort of*
sub	*under, beneath*
tacitus, tacita, tacitum	*silent, quiet*
tantus, tanta, tantum	*so great, such a great*

An eagle and other standards.

IMPERIUM

STAGE 28

post mortem Cogidubnī, Salvius rēgnum eius occupāvit.
pecūniam ā Britannīs extorquēre statim coepit. Salvium
adiuvābat Belimicus, prīnceps Canticōrum.

    prope aulam habitābat agricola Britannicus, quī Salviō
pecūniam trādere nōluit. Salvius igitur mīlitibus imperāvit ut
casam agricolae dīriperent. centuriōnem mīlitibus praefēcit.

the gladiator's sword

1 mīlitēs, gladiīs hastīsque armātī, casam
agricolae oppugnāvērunt.

2 agricola, gladiō centuriōnis vulnerātus,
exanimātus dēcidit.

nablative:
with /by/ from
(sometimes)
in

3 servī, clāmōribus territī,
fūgērunt. by the shouts

4   fīlius agricolae, fūste armātus, frūstrā
     restitit.

5   Belimicus spē praemiī adductus, mīlitēs
     Rōmānōs adiuvābat et incitābat.

6   mīlitēs casam intrāvērunt et arcam,
     pecūniā complētam, abstulērunt.

7   deinde mīlitēs fēminās, catēnīs vīnctās, ad
castra dūxērunt.

8   postrēmō mīlitēs casam incendērunt.
flammae, ventō auctae, casam celeriter
cōnsūmpsērunt.

9   pāstōrēs, quī prope casam habitābant, immōtī stābant,
spectāculō attonitī.
    casam vīdērunt, flammīs cōnsūmptam.
    filium agricolae vīdērunt, hastā graviter vulnerātum.
    agricolam ipsum vīdērunt, gladiō centuriōnis interfectum.
    tandem abiērunt, īrā commōtī, Belimicum Rōmānōsque
vituperantēs.

testāmentum

ego, Tiberius Claudius Cogidubnus, rēx magnus Britannōrum,
morbō gravī afflīctus, hoc testāmentum fēcī.

ego Titum Flāvium Domitiānum, optimum Imperātōrum,
hērēdem meum faciō. mandō T. Flāviō Domitiānō rēgnum
meum cīvēsque Rēgnēnsēs. iubeō cīvēs Rēgnēnsēs lēgibus
pārēre et vītam quiētam agere. *border*
obeys dō lēgō Cn Iūliō Agricolae statuam meam, ā fabrō Britannicō
act
factam. sīc Agricola mē per tōtam vītam in memoriā habēre
potest. *Cnaeus*

dō lēgō C. Salviō Līberālī, fidēlissimō amīcōrum meōrum,
duōs tripodas argenteōs. Salvius vir summae prūdentiae est.

dō lēgō L. Marciō Memorī vīllam meam prope Aquās Sūlis
sitam. L. Marcius Memor, ubi aeger ad thermās vēnī, ut
auxilium ā deā Sūle peterem, benignē mē excēpit.

dō lēgō Dumnorigī, prīncipī Rēgnēnsium, quem sīcut fīlium
amāvī, mīlle aureōs aulamque meam. sī forte Dumnorix
mortuus est, haec C. Salviō Līberālī lēgō.

dō lēgō Belimicō, prīncipī Canticōrum, quīngentōs aureōs et
nāvem celerrimam. Belimicus enim mē ab ursā ōlim servāvit,
quae per aulam meam saeviēbat.

mandō C. Salviō Līberālī cūram fūneris meī. volō Salvium
corpus meum sepelīre. volō eum mēcum sepelīre gemmās meās,
paterās aureās, omnia arma quae ad bellum vēnātiōnemque
comparāvī.

mandō C. Salviō Līberālī hoc testāmentum, manū meā
scrīptum ānulōque meō signātum. dolus malus ab hōc
testāmentō abestō!

5

hērēdem: hērēs *heir*
mandō: mandāre *order,*
  entrust
lēgibus: lēx *law*
lēgō: lēgāre *bequeath*
sīc *thus, in this way*
in memoriā habēre *keep in*
  mind, remember

10

15

benignē *kindly*
excēpit: excipere *receive*
mīlle *a thousand*

quīngentōs: quīngentī *five*
  hundred
20
celerrimam: celer *quick, fast*
fūneris: fūnus *funeral*
sepelīre *bury*
gemmās: gemma *gem, jewel*
ad bellum *for war*
25
signātum: signāre *sign, seal*
dolus … abestō! *may …*
  trickery keep away!
malus *evil, bad*

in aulā Salviī

When you have read this story, answer the questions at the end.

Salvius, cum dē morte Cogidubnī audīvisset, ē castrīs discessit.
per prōvinciam iter fēcit ad aulam quam ē testāmentō accēperat.
ibi novem diēs manēbat ut rēs Cogidubnī administrāret. decimō
diē, iterum profectus, pecūniam opēsque ā Britannīs extorquēre
incēpit. nōnnūllī prīncipēs, avāritiā et metū corruptī, Salvium   5
adiuvābant.

    Belimicus, quamquam multa praemia honōrēsque ā Salviō
accēpit, haudquāquam contentus erat. rēx enim Rēgnēnsium
esse cupiēbat. hāc spē adductus, cum paucīs prīncipibus
coniūrāre coepit. quī tamen, Belimicō diffīsī, rem Salviō   10
rettulērunt.

    Salvius, audāciā Belimicī incēnsus, eum interficere cōnstituit.
amīcōs igitur, quibus maximē cōnfīdēbat, ad sē vocāvit; eōs in
aulam ingressōs rogāvit utrum vim an venēnum adhibēret.

    ūnus ex amīcīs, vir callidissimus,   15
    'venēnum', inquit, 'Belimicō, hostī īnfestō, aptissimum est.'

    'sed quō modō tālem rem efficere possumus?' inquit Salvius.
'nam Belimicus, vir magnae prūdentiae, nēminī cōnfīdit.'

    'hunc homunculum dēcipere nōbīs facile est', inquit ille.
'venēnum cibō mixtum multōs virōs callidiōrēs quam   20
Belimicum iam fefellit. ipse sciō venēnum perītē dare.'

    'euge!' inquit Salvius, cōnsiliō amīcī dēlectātus. 'facillimum
est mihi illum ad cēnam sūmptuōsam invītāre. necesse est mihi
epistulam blandam eī mittere. verbīs enim mollibus ac blandīs
resistere nōn potest.'   25

    Salvius igitur Belimicum ad aulam sine morā invītāvit. quī,
epistulā mendācī dēceptus neque ūllam fraudem suspicātus, ad
aulam nōnā hōrā vēnit.

---

decimō: decimus *tenth*
profectus *having set out*
avāritiā: avāritia *greed*
metū: metus *fear*

haudquāquam *not at all*
spē: spēs *hope*
adductus: addūcere *lead on, encourage*
rettulērunt: referre *tell, report*
audāciā: audācia *boldness, audacity*
incēnsus *inflamed, angered*
utrum … an *whether … or*
adhibēret: adhibēre *use*
īnfestō: īnfestus *dangerous*
aptissimum: aptus *suitable*
mixtum: miscēre *mix*
fefellit: fallere *deceive*
sūmptuōsam: sūmptuōsus *expensive, lavish*
blandam: blandus *flattering*
mollibus: mollis *soft*
morā: mora *delay*
neque *and not*
ūllam: ūllus *any*
fraudem: fraus *trick*
nōnā: nōnus *ninth*

Questions

1 Where was Salvius when he heard of Cogidubnus' death?
   Where did he then travel to (lines 1–2)? 2
2 How long did Salvius stay there? Why? 2
3 After setting out again, what did Salvius do next (lines 3–5)? 1
4 What motivated some chieftains to help him? 1
5 Why would you have expected Belimicus to be satisfied? Why
   did he start plotting (lines 7–10)? 2
6 How did Salvius find out about Belimicus' plot (lines 10–11)? 1
7 What decision did Salvius take when he heard of Belimicus'
   treachery? What question did Salvius put to his friends? 2
8 What did one of the friends suggest? Why did Salvius feel
   doubtful about it? 2
9 The friend gave reasons in support of his suggestion (lines 19–21).
   Give two of them. 2
10 What did Salvius say would be very easy to do (lines 22–3)? 1
11 How did Salvius say he would lure Belimicus into his trap?
    Why was he certain of success (lines 23–5)? 2
12 Pick out and translate one group of Latin words in the last
    sentence to show that Belimicus fell into the trap. 2

TOTAL **20**

About the language 1: the ablative case

1   Study the following sentences:

Britannī, **tantā iniūriā** incēnsī, sēditiōnem fēcērunt.
The Britons, angered by such great injustice, revolted.

iuvenis, **gladiō** armātus, ad castra contendit.
The young man, armed with a sword, hurried to the camp.

mīles, **vulnere** impedītus, tandem cessit.
The soldier, hindered by his wound, gave in at last.

servī, **catēnīs** vīnctī, in fundō labōrābant.
The slaves, bound with chains, were working on the farm.

cīvēs, **clāmōribus** excitātī, ē lectīs surrēxērunt.
The citizens, awakened by the shouts, rose from their beds.

The words in **bold type** are in the ablative case

2   Compare the nominative singular with the ablative singular and ablative plural
    in the first, second and third declensions:

	nominative singular	*ablative singular*	*ablative plural*
first declension	puella	puellā	puellīs
second declension	servus	servō	servīs
	puer	puerō	puerīs
	templum	templō	templīs
third declension	mercātor	mercātōre	mercātōribus
	leō	leōne	leōnibus
	rēx	rēge	rēgibus
	nōmen	nōmine	nōminibus

3   Further examples:

a   Salvius, audāciā Belimicī attonitus, nihil dīxit.
b   mercātor, fūstibus verberātus, in fossā exanimātus iacēbat.
c   mīlitēs, mūrō dēfēnsī, barbarīs diū resistēbant.
d   uxor mea ānulum, gemmīs ōrnātum, ēmit.
e   hospitēs, arte ancillae dēlectātī, plausērunt.

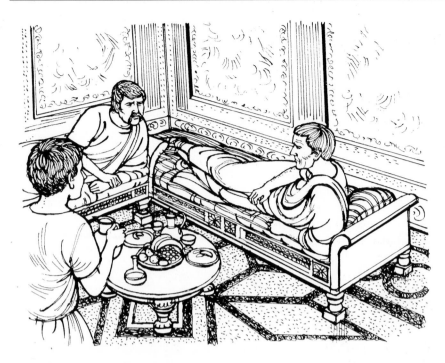

cēna Salviī

Belimicum aulam intrantem Salvius benignē excēpit et in triclīnium addūxit. ibi sōlī sūmptuōsē atque hilarē cēnābant. Belimicus, Salvium rīdentem cōnspicātus vīnōque solūtus, audācter dīcere coepit:

'mī Salvī, multa et magna beneficia ā mē accēpistī. postquam 5
effūgērunt Quīntus et Dumnorix, ego sōlus tē adiūvī; multōs continuōs diēs eōs persecūtus, Dumnorigem occīdī; multa falsa Agricolae dīxī ut Cogidubnum perfidiae damnārem. prō hīs tantīs beneficiīs praemium meritum rogō.'

Salvius, ubi haec audīvit, arrogantiā Belimicī incēnsus, īram 10
tamen cēlāvit et cōmiter respondit:

'praemium meritum iam tibi parāvī. sed cūr nihil cōnsūmis, mī amīce? volō tē garum exquīsītissimum gustāre quod ex Hispāniā importāvī. puer! fer mihi et Belimicō illud garum!'

cum servus garum ambōbus dedisset, Salvius ad hospitem 15
versus,

'dīc mihi, Belimice', inquit, 'quid prō hīs tantīs beneficiīs repetis?'

'iam ex testāmentō Cogidubnī', respondit ille, 'quīngentōs aureōs accēpī. id haudquāquam satis est. rēgnum ipsum repetō.' 20

quod cum audīvisset, Salvius 'ego', inquit, 'nōn Cogidubnus, aureōs tibi dedī. cūr haud satis est?'

'quid dīcis?' exclāmāvit Belimicus. 'hoc nōn intellegō.'

'illud testāmentum', respondit Salvius, 'est falsum. nōn Cogidubnus sed ego scrīpsī.' 25

addūxit: addūcere *lead*
sūmptuōsē *lavishly*
atque *and*
hilarē *in high spirits*
vīnō ... solūtus *relaxed by the wine*
audācter *boldly*
persecūtus *having pursued*
damnārem: damnāre *condemn*
meritum: meritus *well-deserved*
īram: īra *anger*
Hispāniā: Hispānia *Spain*

repetis: repetere *claim*

haud *not*

About the language 2: expressions of time

1 Study the following examples:

> lēgātus sermōnem cum Quīntō **duās hōrās** habēbat.
> *The commander talked with Quintus for two hours.*

> **quattuor diēs** fugitīvus in silvā latēbat.
> *For four days, the fugitive lay hidden in the wood.*

In each of these sentences, the words in **bold type** indicate how long something went on; for this, Latin uses the accusative case.

2 Now study the following:

> **tertiā hōrā** nūntiī advēnērunt.
> *At the third hour, the messengers arrived.*

> **decimō diē** Agricola pugnāre cōnstituit.
> *On the tenth day, Agricola decided to fight.*

In these sentences, the words in **bold type** indicate when something happened; for this, Latin uses the ablative case.

3 Further examples:

a hospitēs trēs hōrās cēnābant.
b quārtō diē revēnit rēx.
c Agricola prōvinciam septem annōs administrāvit.
d secundā hōrā lībertus Memorem excitāre temptāvit.
e mediā nocte hostēs castra nostra oppugnāvērunt.
f sex diēs nāvigābāmus; septimō diē ad portum advēnimus.

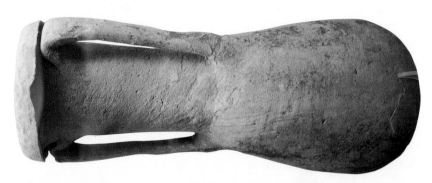

An amphora that brought garum from Spain to Chester.

Belimicus rēx

Belimicus, cum haec audīvisset, adeō attonitus erat ut nihil respondēre posset. Salvius autem haec addidit rīdēns,
'mī amīce, cūr tam attonitus es? tū et Cogidubnus semper inimīcī erātis. num quicquam ab illō spērāvistī? nōs autem in amīcitiā sumus. tibi multum dēbeō, ut dīxistī. itaque rēgem tē creāre in animō habeō. sed rēgnum quod tibi dēstinō multō maius est quam Cogidubnī. heus! puer! plūs garī!'
servus, cui Salvius hoc imperāvit, statim exiit. brevī regressus, garum venēnō mixtum intulit atque in Belimicī pateram effūdit. tam laetus erat ille, ubi verba Salviī audīvit, ut garum cōnsūmeret, ignārus perīculī mortis.
'quantum est hoc rēgnum quod mihi prōmīsistī? ubi gentium est?' rogāvit Belimicus.
Salvius cachinnāns 'multō maius est', inquit, 'quam imperium Rōmānum.'
Belimicus hīs verbīs permōtus,
'nimium bibistī, mī amīce', inquit. 'nūllum rēgnum nōvī maius quam imperium Rōmānum.'
'rēgnum est, quō omnēs tandem abeunt', respondit Salvius. 'rēgnum est, unde nēmō redīre potest. Belimice, tē rēgem creō mortuōrum.'
Belimicus, metū mortis pallidus, surrēxit. haerēbat lingua in gutture; tintinābant aurēs. ventrem, quī iam graviter dolēbat, prēnsāvit. metū īrāque commōtus exclāmāvit,
'tū mihi nocēre nōn audēs, quod omnia scelera tua Agricolae dēnūntiāre possum.'
'mē dēnūntiāre nōn potes, Belimice, quod nunc tibi imminet mors. nunc tibi abeundum est in rēgnum tuum. avē atque valē, mī Belimice!' ← gerundive
Belimicus, venēnō excruciātus, magnum gemitum dedit et humī cecidit mortuus. servī corpus Belimicī ē triclīniō extractum in hortō incendērunt. flammae, ventō auctae, corpus celerrimē cōnsūmpsērunt. sīc Belimicus arrogantiae poenās dedit; sīc Salvius cēterīs prīncipibus persuāsit ut in fidē manērent.

spērāvistī: spērāre hope, expect
amīcitiā: amīcitia friendship
creāre make, create
dēstinō: dēstināre intend

effūdit: effundere pour out

ubi gentium? where in the world?

lingua tongue
gutture: guttur throat
tintinābant: tintināre ring
ventrem: venter stomach
graviter dolēbat: graviter dolēre be extremely painful
scelera: scelus crime
dēnūntiāre denounce, reveal
imminet: imminēre hang over
tibi abeundum est you must go away
avē atque valē hail and farewell
excruciātus: excruciāre torture, torment
ventō: ventus wind
auctae: augēre increase

Duck is trousers for a body

About the language 3: prepositions

1   From Stage 1 onwards, you have met phrases of the following kind:

ad fundum	**ex** ātriō	**per** viās	**cum** amīcīs
to the farm	*out of the hall*	*through the streets*	*with friends*

The words in **bold type** are prepositions. A preposition is normally used with a noun in the accusative or ablative case.

2   The prepositions **ad**, **per** and **prope** are used with the accusative:

ad **rēgem**	per **flammās**	prope **sellam**
to the king	*through the flames*	*near the chair*

Other prepositions used with the accusative are:

ante	inter	circum	post
before,	*between,*	*around*	*after, behind*
in front of	*among*		

contrā	trāns	extrā
against	*across*	*outside*

3   The prepositions **ā**, **ab**, **cum**, **ē** and **ex** are used with the ablative:

ab **amphitheātrō**	ex **oppidō**	cum **hospitibus**
from the amphitheatre	*out of the town*	*with the guests*

Other prepositions used with the ablative are:

dē	prō	sine
down from,	*in front of,*	*without*
about	*in return for,*	
	on behalf of	

4   Further examples:

  a   duo amīcī ad urbem iter faciēbant.
  b   prope templum deae erat fōns sacer.
  c   prīncipēs dē morte Belimicī sermōnem habēbant.
  d   prō aulā stābant quattuor custōdēs.
  e   centuriō sine mīlitibus revēnit.
  f   nauta nāvem circum saxum dīrēxit.
  g   inter Rōmānōs et hostēs erat flūmen altum.
  h   Modestus contrā barbarōs pugnāre nōlēbat.

5 Notice how the preposition **in** is used:

cīvēs **in forum** cucurrērunt.
*The citizens ran **into the forum**.*
mercātōrēs **in forō** negōtium agēbant.
*The merchants were doing business **in the forum**.*

in meaning *into* or *onto* is used with the accusative.
in meaning *in* or *on* is used with the ablative.

Further examples:

a ancilla centuriōnem in tabernam dūxit.
b canis in mēnsam īnsiluit.
c mīlitēs in castrīs labōrābant.
d erat in monte templum splendidum.

Word patterns: adjectives and nouns

1 Study the form and meaning of the following adjectives and nouns:

avārus	*greedy, miserly*	avāritia	*greed*
laetus	*happy*	laetitia	*happiness*
īnsānus	*mad*	īnsānia	*madness*

2 Now complete the table below:

superbus	*proud*	superbia	....
trīstis	....	trīstitia	....
perītus	....	perītia	*skill, experience*
prūdēns	*shrewd, sensible*	prūdentia	....
sapiēns	....	....	....
ēlegāns	....	ēlegantia	....

3 Give the meaning of the following nouns:

audācia, amīcitia, arrogantia, potentia, perfidia

Practising the language

1 Complete each of the sentences below with the correct person of the subjunctive verb. Then translate the sentence. For example:

> tam perterritī erāmus ut ex urbe fugerē… .
> tam perterritī erāmus ut ex urbe **fugerēmus**.
> *We were so frightened that we fled from the city.*

a Quīntus nesciēbat quō modō Cogidubnus periisse… .
b cīvēs, cum tabernam intrāvisse…, vīnum poposcērunt.
c Agricola mīlitibus imperāvit ut ad castra redīre… .
d tantus erat clāmor ut nēmō centuriōnem audīre… .
e nōs, cum Agricolam vīdissē…, maximē gaudēbāmus.
f rēxne tibi persuāsit ut sēcum templum vīsitārē… ?
g domum rediī ut parentēs meōs adiuvāre… .
h cūr dīcere nōlēbātis ubi illō diē mātrem vestram vīdissē… ?

2 Complete each sentence with the correct ablative from the box below. Then translate the sentence.

> audāciā   vīnō   gladiō   fūstibus   īrā   catēnīs

a nūntius, ... graviter vulnerātus, effugere nōn poterat.
b Salvius, ... eius attonitus, diū tacēbat.
c captīvī, ... vīnctī, in longīs ōrdinibus stābant.
d Britannī, ... armātī, pugnāre volēbant.
e dominus, ... commōtus, omnēs servōs carnificibus trādidit.
f hospitēs, ... solūtī, clāmāre et iocōs facere coepērunt.

Interpreting the evidence: our knowledge of Roman Britain

Our knowledge of the Roman occupation of Britain is based on different types of evidence:

1 *literary* evidence: what the Greeks and Romans wrote about Britain;
2 *archaeological* evidence: what archaeologists have discovered from excavations, including:
3 *inscriptional* evidence: inscriptions in Latin (and sometimes Greek) from tombstones, altars, public buildings and monuments, and from private objects such as writing-tablets, defixiones etc.

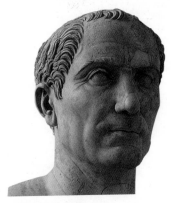

Julius Caesar.

Literary evidence

A picture of Roman Britain is given in two well-known Latin texts. One is Julius Caesar's account of his brief reconnaissance mission to the Kent coast in 55 BC and his return in greater force the following year when he stormed the fortress of a British king before withdrawing again. The other is Tacitus' biography of his father-in-law, Agricola. Much of this is devoted to Agricola's career in the army in Roman Britain and to his campaigns as governor of the province. The account of Agricola's life in Stage 26 is almost entirely based on Tacitus' description.

Both pieces of writing are to some extent biased. Caesar wrote his account in order to justify his actions to the Senate in Rome and place himself in a favourable light; Tacitus was anxious to honour the memory of his father-in-law and to praise his success as governor and a soldier. Agricola appears almost too good to be true, in strong contrast to the Emperor Domitian who is portrayed as jealous of his success and anxious to bring about his downfall.

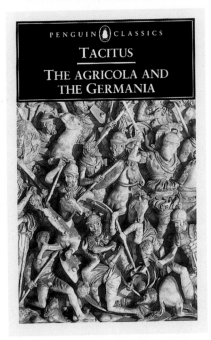

Tacitus' Agricola *in an English translation.*

A rescue excavation: a Roman military bath house at Catterick in North Yorkshire. This excavation was undertaken during the construction of a new bypass, seen in the background.

Archaeological evidence

The task of archaeologists is to uncover and explain the remains of the past. First they must locate a suitable site to excavate. Some sites are already known but have not been completely excavated; others are found by accident. In 1960 a workman digging a drain came across fragments of a mosaic floor and this chance discovery led to the excavation of the palace at Fishbourne. When sites are needed for road building or other kinds of development, archaeologists may have limited time in which to excavate before the bulldozers move in or the remains are reburied.

Once the site has been located, archaeologists have to plan and carry out a careful scientific survey and excavation of the area. As the earth is removed from a site, they will watch for two things: the existence and position of any foundations, and the way in which the various levels or layers of earth change colour and texture. In this way they build up a picture of the main features on the site.

At the same time they carefully examine the soil for smaller pieces of evidence such as bones, pottery, jewellery, coins and other small objects. The aim is not simply to find precious objects but to discover as much as possible about the people who used the buildings, what their life was like, when they lived there and

Excavating a Roman well. The excavation was undertaken before the site was destroyed by gravel extraction.

even perhaps what happened to them. For such work the archaeologist needs some of the same kind of training and skills as a detective.

Roman coins can usually be accurately dated because they have emperors' heads and names stamped on them. These in turn can help date the level of soil being excavated. Fairly accurate dates can also be obtained from a study of the styles and patterns of pottery found on a site. Large quantities have survived, as pottery is a durable material which does not rot, and broken pieces (sherds) are found in very large numbers on many sites. The presence on a British site of pottery which has

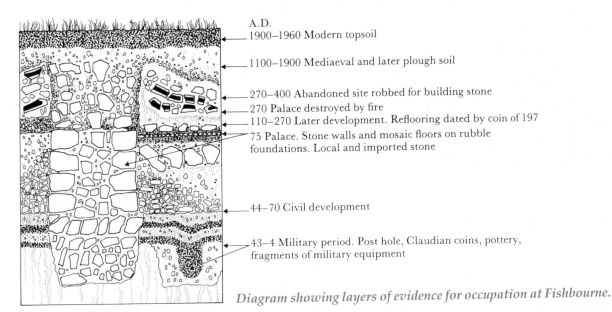

A.D.
1900–1960 Modern topsoil

1100–1900 Mediaeval and later plough soil

270–400 Abandoned site robbed for building stone
270 Palace destroyed by fire
110–270 Later development. Reflooring dated by coin of 197
75 Palace. Stone walls and mosaic floors on rubble foundations. Local and imported stone

44–70 Civil development

43–4 Military period. Post hole, Claudian coins, pottery, fragments of military equipment

Diagram showing layers of evidence for occupation at Fishbourne.

A field belonging to a Roman villa at Wollaston, Northamptonshire, was found to contain a system of trenches. Very careful attention to differences of colour and texture in the soil revealed a planting trench with holes at the sides for posts to support the plants. Microscopic examination of pollen in the trench showed that these were grape vines.

come from Italy or Gaul shows that the owner was wealthy enough to pay for imported goods. In ways such as this archaeologists can begin to assemble information about the people who occupied the site.

By such painstaking processes archaeologists have been able to reconstruct a remarkably detailed picture of the Roman occupation of Britain. Many sites in Britain show a gradual development from a simple timber-framed farmhouse building, which was replaced by a larger stone house, to a grander, multi-roomed mansion with baths, mosaic pavements and colonnades. The fact that most of the Romano-British villas were sited in the south-east, whereas the military fortresses were established in the north and west, suggests that Britain was largely peaceful and prosperous in the south-east but still troubled by the threat of hostile tribes in the north-west. Traces of a vast network of Roman roads have been found, showing just how numerous and effective communications must have been. Parts of many Romano-British towns have been excavated, for example, London, Bath, Wroxeter, St Albans and Silchester, which reveal how advanced urban life was. It is not uncommon to find the remains of an extensive forum, carefully laid-out grids of streets, the foundations of many large buildings including temples with altars and inscriptions, sometimes a theatre and an amphitheatre, and substantial city walls.

The excavation of military sites, such as forts, marching camps and legionary fortresses, has shown how important the army was in maintaining peace and protecting the province from tribes in Scotland and in north and west Wales. It has also shown very clearly the movements of the legions and auxiliaries around the country and told us much about the lives of Roman soldiers.

Finds of coins and pottery are useful in dating levels, but need careful interpretation. This denarius of the Emperor Vespasian, who sent Agricola to govern Britain, was minted in AD 73. But coins circulated for many years; this was found with other coins issued a century later.

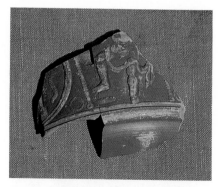

This small fragment of a pottery bowl can be dated by the style of decoration. It was made in central Gaul about AD 240–270. However, it would have been an expensive import and so could have been treasured for generations before it eventually broke and was thrown away.

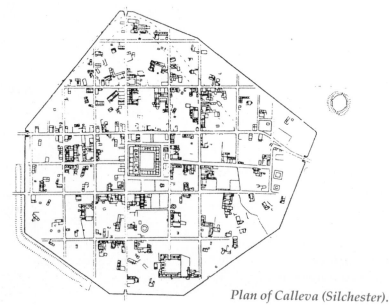

Plan of Calleva (Silchester).

Britain in the later first century AD

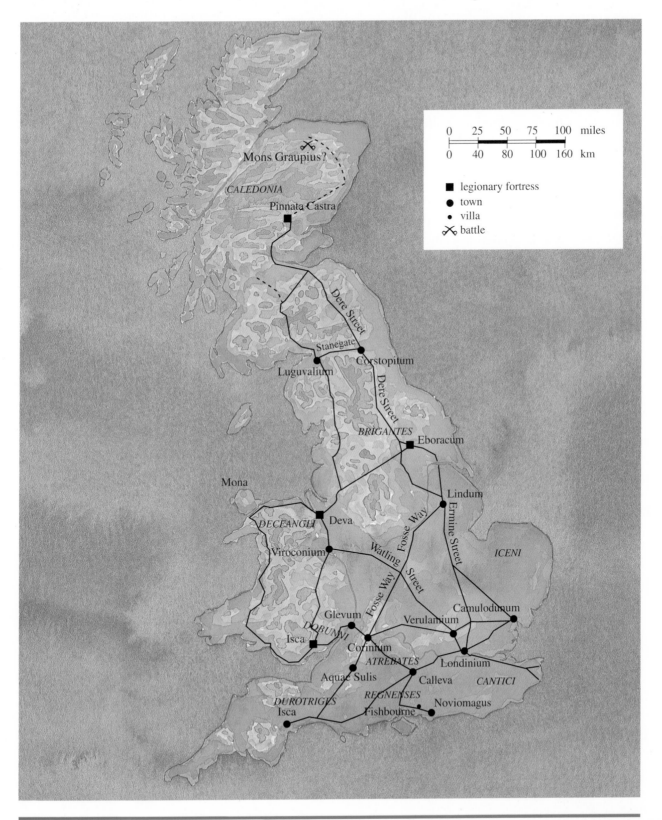

Mons Graupius?

CALEDONIA

Pinnata Castra

0 25 50 75 100 miles
0 40 80 100 160 km

■ legionary fortress
● town
• villa
⚔ battle

Dere Street

Stanegate
Corstopitum
Luguvalium

Dere Street

BRIGANTES
Eboracum

Mona

Lindum

DECEANGLI Deva

ICENI

Viroconium

Watling
Street

Fosse Way

Ermine Street

Glevum
Verulamium
Camulodunum

Fosse Way

DOBUNNI
Isca
Corinium
Londinium
ATREBATES
Aquae Sulis
Calleva
CANTICI
DUROTRIGES
REGNENSES
Isca
Fishbourne
Noviomagus

Inscriptional evidence

Some important evidence about the Roman occupation of Britain comes from inscriptions, particularly on the tombstones of soldiers. On the right is the inscription on the tombstone of a soldier who was buried at Chester.

At first sight, this looks difficult to decipher. The task, however, is made easier by the fact that most of these inscriptions follow a standard pattern. The items are usually arranged in the following order:

> D M
> L LICINIUS L F
> TER VALENS
> ARE VETERAN
> LEG XX VV AN VL
> H S E

1   The dedication at the top of the stone – D M – abbreviation for **Dīs Mānibus**, the spirits of the departed.
2   The praenomen. This is the first of a citizen's three names and is usually abbreviated to a single letter, as here – L for **Lūcius**.
3   The nomen. Always given in full, as here – **Licinius**.
4   The father's name. It is usually only the father's praenomen that is given, and this can be recognised in abbreviated form by the single letter which comes before an F representing **fīlius**. The son often had the same praenomen as his father, as here – L F for **Lūciī fīlius**.
5   Tribe. Roman soldiers were Roman citizens and were therefore enrolled in one of the thirty-five Roman tribes which were used for voting purposes. The name of the tribe is abbreviated, as here – TER for **Teretīna**.
6   The cognomen. This is the last of the three names, usually placed after the father's name and the Roman tribe in which the soldier was enrolled. It is always given in full, as here – **Valēns**. Three names were a mark of Roman citizenship and therefore an important indication of status.
7   Birthplace. This can usually be identified as a town in the Roman empire, thus ARE for **Arelātē** (modern Arles in the south of France).
8   Rank and legion. They are usually both abbreviated – VETERAN for **veterānus** (a retired soldier or one coming up to retirement); LEG XX VV for **legiōnis XX Valeriae Victrīcis** (20th Legion Valeria Victrix).
9   Age. This is represented by AN or ANN for **annōrum**, followed by a number. This number is in most cases rounded off to a multiple of 5. Sometimes VIX (**vīxit** = lived) is placed before AN.
10 Length of service (not included in the inscription above). This is represented by STIP followed by a number, e.g. STIP X for **stipendia X** (ten years' service).
11 The final statement. This is abbreviated, and usually takes the form of H S E for **hīc situs est** (is buried here) or H F C for **hērēs faciendum cūrāvit** (his heir had this stone set up).

The Chester inscription can therefore be interpreted as follows:

> D(IS) M(ANIBUS)
> L(UCIUS) LICINIUS L(UCII) F(ILIUS)
> TER(ETINA) VALENS
> ARE(LATE) VETERAN(US)
> LEG(IONIS) XXV(ALERIAE) V(ICTRICIS) AN(NORUM)
> V L
> H(IC) S(ITUS) E(ST)

This stone is dedicated to the spirits of the departed. Lucius Licinius Valens, son of Lucius, of the Teretine tribe, from Arelate, veteran of the Twentieth Legion Valeria Victrix, aged 45, is buried here.

On the right is the inscription on another soldier's tombstone, also found at Chester.

Try to find out from it the following information:

1 The soldier's name
2 His rank
3 His legion
4 His age at death
5 The length of his service

In the same way, find as much information as you can from the following inscription:

Vocabulary checklist 28

ac	*and*
atque	*and*
cōnstituō, cōnstituere, cōnstituī, cōnstitūtus	*decide*
corpus, corporis	*body*
doleō, dolēre, doluī	*hurt, be in pain*
gemitus, gemitūs	*groan*
īra, īrae	*anger*
malus, mala, malum	*evil, bad*
mandō, mandāre, mandāvī, mandātus	*entrust, hand over*
metus, metūs	*fear*
occīdō, occīdere, occīdī, occīsus	*kill*
opēs, opum	*money, wealth*
quicquam (*also spelt* quidquam)	*anything*
sīc	*thus, in this way*
spēs, speī	*hope*
suspicātus, suspicāta, suspicātum	*having suspected*
ut	*as*
ventus, ventī	*wind*

ūnus	*one*
duo	*two*
trēs	*three*
quattuor	*four*
quīnque	*five*
sex	*six*
septem	*seven*
octō	*eight*
novem	*nine*
decem	*ten*
vīgintī	*twenty*
trīgintā	*thirty*
quadrāgintā	*forty*
quīnquāgintā	*fifty*
sexāgintā	*sixty*
septuāgintā	*seventy*
octōgintā	*eighty*
nōnāgintā	*ninety*
centum	*a hundred*
mīlle	*a thousand*
mīlia	*thousands*

An altar at Chester dedicated to the Holy Genius (Guardian Spirit) of his century by Aelius Claudianus, optio. VS stands for **VOTVM SOLVIT**, *'fulfilled his vow'. Aelius had promised to set up the altar if a prayer of his was answered. (Modern copy.)*

LANGUAGE INFORMATION

Contents

Part One: About the language   **146**

Nouns   146

Adjectives   148

Comparatives and superlatives   150

Pronouns I   152
    ego, tū, nōs, vōs, sē

Pronouns II   153
    hic, ille, is, ipse

Pronouns III   155
    quī

Verbs   156

Irregular verbs   158

Uses of the cases   160

Uses of the participle   161

Uses of the subjunctive   163

Word order   165

Longer sentences   166

Part Two: Vocabulary   **168**

Part One: About the language

Nouns

1

	first declension	second declension		
GENDER	f.	m.	m.	n.
SINGULAR				
nominative and vocative	puella	servus (*voc.* serve)	puer	templum
accusative	puellam	servum	puerum	templum
genitive (of)	puellae	servī	puerī	templī
dative (to, for)	puellae	servō	puerō	templō
ablative (by, with)	puellā	servō	puerō	templō
PLURAL				
nominative and vocative	puellae	servī	puerī	templa
accusative	puellās	servōs	puerōs	templa
genitive (of)	puellārum	servōrum	puerōrum	templōrum
dative (to, for)	puellīs	servīs	puerīs	templīs
ablative (by, with)	puellīs	servīs	puerīs	templīs

2 Study the following nouns:

	fourth declension		fifth declension
GENDER	f.	n.	m.
SINGULAR			
nominative and vocative	manus	genū	diēs
accusative	manum	genū	diem
genitive (of)	manūs	genūs	diēī
dative (to, for)	manuī	genū	diēī
ablative (by, with)	manū	genū	diē
PLURAL			
nominative and vocative	manūs	genua	diēs
accusative	manūs	genua	diēs
genitive (of)	manuum	genuum	diērum
dative (to, for)	manibus	genibus	diēbus
ablative (by, with)	manibus	genibus	diēbus

third declension						
m.	m.	m.	m.	f.	n.	GENDER
						SINGULAR
mercātor	leō	cīvis	rēx	urbs	nōmen	*nominative and vocative*
mercātōrem	leōnem	cīvem	rēgem	urbem	nōmen	*accusative*
mercātōris	leōnis	cīvis	rēgis	urbis	nōminis	*genitive (of)*
mercātōrī	leōnī	cīvī	rēgī	urbī	nōminī	*dative (to, for)*
mercātōre	leōne	cīve	rēge	urbe	nōmine	*ablative (by, with)*
						PLURAL
mercātōrēs	leōnēs	cīvēs	rēgēs	urbēs	nōmina	*nominative and vocative*
mercātōrēs	leōnēs	cīvēs	rēgēs	urbēs	nōmina	*accusative*
mercātōrum	leōnum	cīvium	rēgum	urbium	nōminum	*genitive (of)*
mercātōribus	leōnibus	cīvibus	rēgibus	urbibus	nōminibus	*dative (to, for)*
mercātōribus	leōnibus	cīvibus	rēgibus	urbibus	nōminibus	*ablative (by, with)*

3   **manus** and **genū** belong to the fourth declension, and **diēs** to the fifth Compare their endings with those of the other declensions. Notice especially the form and pronunciation of the genitive singular, nominative plural and accusative plural of **manus**.

4   With the help of the table opposite, find the Latin for the words in *italic type* in the following sentences:

   a   Seven *days* had now passed.
   b   The priest raised his *hand*.
   c   The injured man's *knees* were very painful.
   d   The mother washed the child's *hands* and face.
   e   It was the sixth hour of the *day*.

5   You have now met all the declensions and cases of the noun. For a summary of the ways in which the different cases are used, see **Uses of the cases** p. 160.

Adjectives

1 The following adjectives belong to the 1st and 2nd declensions:

SINGULAR	*masculine*	*feminine*	*neuter*	*masculine*	*feminine*	*neuter*
nominative and vocative	bonus (voc. bone)	bona	bonum	pulcher	pulchra	pulchrum
accusative	bonum	bonam	bonum	pulchrum	pulchram	pulchrum
genitive	bonī	bonae	bonī	pulchrī	pulchrae	pulchrī
dative	bonō	bonae	bonō	pulchrō	pulchrae	pulchrō
PLURAL						
nominative and vocative	bonī	bonae	bona	pulchrī	pulchrae	pulchra
accusative	bonōs	bonās	bona	pulchrōs	pulchrās	pulchra
genitive	bonōrum	bonārum	bonōrum	pulchrōrum	pulchrārum	pulchrōrum
dative	bonīs	bonīs	bonīs	pulchrīs	pulchrīs	pulchrīs

2 The following adjectives belong to the 3rd declension:

SINGULAR	*masculine and feminine*	*neuter*	*masculine and feminine*	*neuter*
nominative and vocative	fortis	forte	ingēns	ingēns
accusative	fortem	forte	ingentem	ingēns
genitive	fortis	fortis	ingentis	ingentis
dative	fortī	fortī	ingentī	ingentī
PLURAL				
nominative and vocative	fortēs	fortia	ingentēs	ingentia
accusative	fortēs	fortia	ingentēs	ingentia
genitive	fortium	fortium	ingentium	ingentium
dative	fortibus	fortibus	ingentibus	ingentibus

3 Using paragraphs 1 and 2, find the Latin for the words in *italic type* in the following sentences. Remember that adjectives agree with nouns in number, gender and case.

a The *beautiful* temple stood in the forum.
b This is the house of a *brave* citizen.
c The craftsmen built three *huge* temples.
d They set up a statue to the *good* girl.

4   Translate the following sentences:

   a   iuvenis leōnem saevum facile superāvit.
   b   sacerdōtēs dīs immortālibus sacrificium obtulērunt.
   c   amīcus nāvem mercātōris probī vīdit.
   d   fēminae sapientēs pecūniam cēlāvērunt.
   e   medicus oculōs mīlitum aegrōrum īnspexit.
   f   aedificium ingēns prope flūmen ēmit.

   Pick out the noun and adjective pair in each sentence and state its number, gender and case.

5   The ablative case of the adjectives will be added in Book IV.

Comparatives and superlatives

1   You have met the following comparative and superlative forms of the adjective:

nominative	*comparative*	*superlative*
longus *long*	longior *longer*	longissimus *very long*
pulcher *beautiful*	pulchrior *more beautiful*	pulcherrimus *very beautiful*
fortis *brave*	fortior *braver*	fortissimus *very brave*
fēlīx *lucky*	fēlīcior *luckier*	fēlīcissimus *very lucky*
prūdēns *shrewd*	prūdentior *shrewder*	prūdentissimus *very shrewd*

Notice the following example:

facilis *easy*	facilior *easier*	facillimus *very easy*

2   Irregular forms:

bonus *good*	melior *better*	optimus *very good, best*
malus *bad*	peior *worse*	pessimus *very bad, worst*
magnus *big*	maior *bigger*	maximus *very big*
parvus *small*	minor *smaller*	minimus *very small*
multus *much*	plūs *more*	plūrimus *very much*

which becomes in the plural:

multī *many*	plūrēs *more*	plūrimī *very many, most*

3   Translate the following examples:

a   'nēmō fortior est quam Modestus', inquit Vilbia.
b   longissima erat pompa, pulcherrima quoque.
c   peior es quam fūr!
d   Salviī vīlla erat minor quam aula Cogidubnī.
e   facillimum erat nōbīs urbem capere.
f   numquam tabernam meliōrem quam tuam vīsitāvī.
g   Memor ad maiōrēs honōrēs ascendere volēbat.
h   in mediō oppidō labōrābant plūrimī fabrī, quī templum maximum exstruēbant.

4   You have also met another way of translating the superlative:

>   Rūfe, prūdentissimus es omnium amīcōrum quōs habeō.
>   *Rufus, you are the shrewdest* (or *most shrewd*) *of all the friends that I have.*

The following examples can be translated in the same way:

a   Bregāns erat stultissimus omnium servōrum quōs Salvius habēbat.
b   omnēs mīlitēs meī sunt fortēs; tū tamen fortissimus es.
c   postrēmō Athēnās vīsitāvimus, pulcherrimam omnium urbium.

Pronouns I: ego, tū, nōs, vōs, sē

1   **ego** and **tū** (*I*, *you*, etc.)

	SINGULAR		PLURAL	
nominative	ego	tū	nōs	vōs
accusative	mē	tē	nōs	vōs
dative	mihi	tibi	nōbīs	vōbīs

mēcum = *with me*   **nōbīscum** = *with us*
tēcum = *with you* (singular)   **vōbīscum** = *with you* (plural)

2   **sē** (*himself, herself, themselves*, etc.)

	SINGULAR	PLURAL
accusative	sē	sē
dative	sibi	sibi

sēcum (*with himself*, etc.) is formed like **mēcum**, **tēcum**, etc. Notice some of the ways it can be translated:

> senātor multōs equitēs sēcum habēbat.
> *The senator had many horsemen with him.*

> Britannī uxōrēs sēcum dūcēbant.
> *The Britons were bringing their wives with them.*

> Agricola sēcum cōgitābat.
> *Agricola thought with himself.*

Or, in more natural English:
> *Agricola thought to himself.*

Pronouns II: hic, ille, is, ipse

1 **hic** (*this*, *these*, etc.)

	SINGULAR *masculine*	*feminine*	*neuter*	PLURAL *masculine*	*feminine*	*neuter*
nominative	hic	haec	hoc	hī	hae	haec
accusative	hunc	hanc	hoc	hōs	hās	haec
genitive	huius	huius	huius	hōrum	hārum	hōrum
dative	huic	huic	huic	hīs	hīs	hīs

2 **ille** (*that*, *those*, etc.; sometimes used with the meaning *he*, *she*, *it*, etc.)

	SINGULAR *masculine*	*feminine*	*neuter*	PLURAL *masculine*	*feminine*	*neuter*
nominative	ille	illa	illud	illī	illae	illa
accusative	illum	illam	illud	illōs	illās	illa
genitive	illīus	illīus	illīus	illōrum	illārum	illōrum
dative	illī	illī	illī	illīs	illīs	illīs

3 **is** (*he*, *she*, *it*, etc.):

	SINGULAR *masculine*	*feminine*	*neuter*	PLURAL *masculine*	*feminine*	*neuter*
nominative	is	ea	id	eī	eae	ea
accusative	eum	eam	id	eōs	eās	ea
genitive	eius	eius	eius	eōrum	eārum	eōrum
dative	eī	eī	eī	eīs	eīs	eīs

4 With the help of paragraphs 1–3, find the Latin for the words in *italic type* in the following sentences. You may need to use the gender information in the table of nouns on pp. 146–7.

    a I have never seen *that* girl before.
    b Guard *those* slaves!
    c *These* lions are dangerous.
    d I hate the noise of *this* city.
    e We shall give the prize to *this* boy.
    f We soon found *her*.
    g Where are the merchants? I want to see *them*.
    h Where is the temple? I want to see *it*.
    i Where is the city? I want to see *it*.
    j I hurried to *his* house.

5 **ipse** (meaning *myself, yourself, himself*, etc., depending on the word it is describing):

| | SINGULAR | | | PLURAL | | |
	masculine	*feminine*	*neuter*	*masculine*	*feminine*	*neuter*
nominative	ipse	ipsa	ipsum	ipsī	ipsae	ipsa
accusative	ipsum	ipsam	ipsum	ipsōs	ipsās	ipsa
genitive	ipsīus	ipsīus	ipsīus	ipsōrum	ipsārum	ipsōrum
dative	ipsī	ipsī	ipsī	ipsīs	ipsīs	ipsīs

domina **ipsa** lacrimābat.
*The mistress **herself** was weeping.*

fēmina mē **ipsum** accūsāvit.
*The woman accused me **myself**.*

amīcus Imperātōris **ipsīus** pecūniam mihi prōmīsit.
*A friend of the Emperor **himself** promised money to me.*

nōs **ipsī** latrōnem vīdimus.
*We **ourselves** saw the robber.*

Further examples:

a ego ipse pugnam vīdī.
b nōs ipsī in templō aderāmus.
c subitō rēgem ipsum audīvimus.
d dea ipsa mihi appāruit.

Pronouns III: quī

1 Notice the genitive and dative singular of the relative pronoun **quī**:

	SINGULAR masculine	feminine	neuter	PLURAL masculine	feminine	neuter
nominative	quī	quae	quod	quī	quae	quae
accusative	quem	quam	quod	quōs	quās	quae
genitive	cuius	cuius	cuius	quōrum	quārum	quōrum
dative	cui	cui	cui	quibus	quibus	quibus

senex cuius vīlla ardēbat vehementer clāmābat.
The old man whose house was on fire was shouting loudly.

mercātor cui sellās mēnsāsque heri vēndidī hodiē revēnit.
The merchant to whom I sold chairs and tables yesterday came back today.

Further examples of the various forms of **quī**:

a   mīlitēs quōs Salvius ēmīsit tandem rediērunt.
b   iuvenis, cuius pater in Graeciā aberat, amīcōs ad cēnam sūmptuōsam invītāvit.
c   pater fīliās, quae in oppidō cum mīlitibus convēnerant, saevissimē pūnīvit.
d   servus, cui sacerdōs signum dederat, duās victimās ad āram dūxit.
e   templum, quod in mediā urbe stābat, saepe vīsitābam.
f   epistulam, quam nūntius tulerat, celeriter lēgī.

2 Sometimes the relative pronoun is used at the *beginning* of a sentence. Study the different ways of translating it:

Salviī amīcī īnsidiās Belimicō parāvērunt. **quī**, nihil suspicātus, ad aulam libenter vēnit.
*Salvius' friends prepared a trap for Belimicus. **He**, having suspected nothing, came willingly to the palace.*

tum mīlitēs intrāvērunt. **quōs** cum vīdisset, servus tremēbat.
*Then the soldiers entered. When he saw **them**, the slave began to tremble.*

Cogidubnus 'grātiās vōbīs agō', inquit. **quod** cum dīxisset, cōnsēdit.
*'Thank you', said Cogidubnus. When he had said **this**, he sat down.*

In examples like these, the relative pronoun is said to be used as a connecting relative

Further examples:

a   'cūr mihi nihil dās?' rogāvit fīlius. quod cum audīvisset, pater īrātissimus erat.
b   mercātor ancillīs pecūniam trādidit. quae, postquam dēnāriōs numerāvērunt, ad vīllam revēnērunt.
c   deinde rēx Memorī signum dedit. quī, togam splendidam gerēns, ad āram sollemniter prōcessit.
d   multī mīlitēs iam aulam complēbant. quōs cum vīdissent, sacerdōtēs surrēxērunt.

Verbs

	first conjugation	second conjugation	third conjugation	fourth conjugation
PRESENT (INDICATIVE)	*I carry, you carry, etc.*	*I teach, you teach, etc.*	*I drag, you drag, etc.*	*I hear, you hear, etc.*
	portō	doceō	trahō	audiō
	portās	docēs	trahis	audīs
	portat	docet	trahit	audit
	portāmus	docēmus	trahimus	audīmus
	portātis	docētis	trahitis	audītis
	portant	docent	trahunt	audiunt
IMPERFECT (INDICATIVE)	*I was carrying*	*I was teaching*	*I was dragging*	*I was hearing*
	portābam	docēbam	trahēbam	audiēbam
	portābās	docēbās	trahēbās	audiēbās
	portābat	docēbat	trahēbat	audiēbat
	portābāmus	docēbāmus	trahēbāmus	audiēbāmus
	portābātis	docēbātis	trahēbātis	audiēbātis
	portābant	docēbant	trahēbant	audiēbant
PERFECT (INDICATIVE)	*I (have) carried*	*I (have) taught*	*I (have) dragged*	*I (have) heard*
	portāvī	docuī	trāxī	audīvī
	portāvistī	docuistī	trāxistī	audīvistī
	portāvit	docuit	trāxit	audīvit
	portāvimus	docuimus	trāximus	audīvimus
	portāvistis	docuistis	trāxistis	audīvistis
	portāvērunt	docuērunt	trāxērunt	audīvērunt
PLUPERFECT (INDICATIVE)	*I had carried*	*I had taught*	*I had dragged*	*I had heard*
	portāveram	docueram	trāxeram	audīveram
	portāverās	docuerās	trāxerās	audīverās
	portāverat	docuerat	trāxerat	audīverat
	portāverāmus	docuerāmus	trāxerāmus	audīverāmus
	portāverātis	docuerātis	trāxerātis	audīverātis
	portāverant	docuerant	trāxerant	audīverant

2 The word indicative is sometimes included in the names of these tenses, to distinguish them from the present subjunctive, imperfect subjunctive, etc.

3   You have also met the following forms of the verb:

	first conjugation	second conjugation	third conjugation	fourth conjugation
INFINITIVE	*to carry* portāre	*to teach* docēre	*to drag* trahere	*to hear* audīre
IMPERATIVE (s.) (pl.)	*carry!* portā portāte	*teach!* docē docēte	*drag!* trahe trahite	*hear!* audī audīte
PRESENT PARTICIPLE	*carrying* portāns	*teaching* docēns	*dragging* trahēns	*hearing* audiēns
PERFECT PASSIVE PARTICIPLE	*(having been) carried* portātus	*(having been) taught* doctus	*(having been) dragged* tractus	*(having been) heard* audītus

4   You have also met some examples of the *perfect active* participle:

locūtus *having spoken*   secūtus *having followed*   ingressus *having entered*

These examples all come from a particular group of verbs. The perfect active participle is the only part of these verbs that you have met so far.

5   For other forms of the present and perfect participles, and for examples of the ways in which they are used, see **Uses of the participle** pp. 161–2.

6   In Stages 24 and 25, you met two tenses of the *subjunctive*:

	first conjugation	second conjugation	third conjugation	fourth conjugation
IMPERFECT SUBJUNCTIVE	portārem portārēs portāret portārēmus portārētis portārent	docērem docērēs docēret docērēmus docērētis docērent	traherem traherēs traheret traherēmus traherētis traherent	audīrem audīrēs audīret audīrēmus audīrētis audīrent
PLUPERFECT SUBJUNCTIVE	portāvissem portāvissēs portāvisset portāvissēmus portāvissētis portāvissent	docuissem docuissēs docuisset docuissēmus docuissētis docuissent	trāxissem trāxissēs trāxisset trāxissēmus trāxissētis trāxissent	audīvissem audīvissēs audīvisset audīvissēmus audīvissētis audīvissent

7   For ways of translating the subjunctive, see **Uses of the subjunctive** pp. 163–4.

Irregular verbs

1 You have now met the following forms of six irregular verbs:

INFINITIVE	*to be* esse	*to be able* posse	*to want* velle	*to bring* ferre	*to go* īre	*to take* capere
PRESENT (INDICATIVE)	*I am* sum es est sumus estis sunt	*I am able* possum potes potest possumus potestis possunt	*I want* volō vīs vult volumus vultis volunt	*I bring* ferō fers fert ferimus fertis ferunt	*I go* eō īs it īmus ītis eunt	*I take* capiō capis capit capimus capitis capiunt
IMPERFECT (INDICATIVE)	*I was* eram erās erat erāmus erātis erant	*I was able* poteram poterās poterat poterāmus poterātis poterant	*I was wanting* volēbam volēbās volēbat volēbāmus volēbātis volēbant	*I was bringing* ferēbam ferēbās ferēbat ferēbāmus ferēbātis ferēbant	*I was going* ībam ībās ībat ībāmus ībātis ībant	*I was taking* capiēbam capiēbās capiēbat capiēbāmus capiēbātis capiēbant
PERFECT (INDICATIVE)	*I have been, was* fuī fuistī fuit fuimus fuistis fuērunt	*I have been, was able* potuī potuistī potuit potuimus potuistis potuērunt	*I (have) wanted* voluī voluistī voluit voluimus voluistis voluērunt	*I (have) brought* tulī tulistī tulit tulimus tulistis tulērunt	*I have gone, went* iī iistī iit iimus iistis iērunt	*I have taken, took* cēpī cēpistī cēpit cēpimus cēpistis cēpērunt
PLUPERFECT (INDICATIVE)	*I had been* fueram fuerās fuerat fuerāmus fuerātis fuerant	*I had been able* potueram potuerās potuerat potuerāmus potuerātis potuerant	*I had wanted* volueram voluerās voluerat voluerāmus voluerātis voluerant	*I had brought* tuleram tulerās tulerat tulerāmus tulerātis tulerant	*I had gone* ieram ierās ierat ierāmus ierātis ierant	*I had taken* cēperam cēperās cēperat cēperāmus cēperātis cēperant

IMPERFECT SUBJUNCTIVE	essem	possem	vellem	ferrem	īrem	caperem
	essēs	possēs	vellēs	ferrēs	īrēs	caperēs
	esset	posset	vellet	ferret	īret	caperet
	essēmus	possēmus	vellēmus	ferrēmus	īrēmus	caperēmus
	essētis	possētis	vellētis	ferrētis	īrētis	caperētis
	essent	possent	vellent	ferrent	īrent	caperent
PLUPERFECT SUBJUNCTIVE	fuissem	potuissem	voluissem	tulissem	iissem	cēpissem
	fuissēs	potuissēs	voluissēs	tulissēs	iissēs	cēpissēs
	fuisset	potuisset	voluisset	tulisset	iisset	cēpisset
	fuissēmus	potuissēmus	voluissēmus	tulissēmus	iissēmus	cēpissēmus
	fuissētis	potuissētis	voluissētis	tulissētis	iissētis	cēpissētis
	fuissent	potuissent	voluissent	tulissent	iissent	cēpissent

2 Give the meaning of the following:

potes; vult; eō; it; fers.
posse; fuī; ībat; capiēbant; tulimus.
cēpistis; fuerāmus; iistis; potuerant; poterant.

3 **capiō** is one of a small group of verbs which belong to the third conjugation but behave in some ways like fourth conjugation verbs. Other common verbs in this group are **accipiō**, **faciō**, **fugiō** and **rapiō**.

Compare the infinitive of **capiō** with the infinitive of **trahō** (third conjugation) on p. 157.

Compare the imperfect (indicative) tense of **capiō** with the imperfect (indicative) tense of **audiō** (fourth conjugation) on p. 156.

Uses of the cases

1 *nominative*
captīvus clāmābat.　　　　　　　*The prisoner was shouting.*

2 *vocative*
valē, **domine**!　　　　　　　*Goodbye, master!*

3 *accusative*
  a **pontem** trānsiimus.　　　*We crossed the bridge.*
  b **trēs hōrās** labōrābam.　　*I was working for three hours.*
  c per **agrōs**; ad **vīllam**　　*through the fields; to the house*

4 *genitive*
  a māter **puerōrum**　　　　*the mother of the boys*
  b plūs **pecūniae**　　　　　*more money*
  c vir **maximae virtūtis**　　*a man of very great courage*

5 *dative*
  a **mīlitibus** cibum dedimus.　*We gave food to the soldiers.*
  b **vestrō candidātō** nōn faveō.　*I do not support your candidate.*

6 *ablative*
  a **spectāculō** attonitus　　　*astonished by the sight*
  b **hastā** armātus　　　　　*armed with a spear*
  c **quārtō diē** revēnit.　　　*He came back on the fourth day.*
  d cum **amīcīs**; ē **tabernā**　*with friends; from the inn*

7 Further examples of some of the uses listed above:
  a Modestus erat homō minimae prūdentiae.
  b multōs annōs ibi habitābam.
  c cūr mihi nōn crēdidistī?
  d satis vīnī bibistī?
  e prīnceps nōmina iuvenum commemorāvit.
  f senex nōbīs fābulam dē morte Caesaris nārrāvit.
  g septimā hōrā discessimus.
  h Belimicus, verbīs Salviī dēceptus, cōnsēnsit.

Uses of the participle

1 In Book II you met the *present participle*:

> parentēs fīliam **cantantem** audīvērunt.
> *The parents heard their daughter **singing**.*

2 In Stage 21 you met the *perfect passive participle*:

> servus, graviter **vulnerātus**, sub plaustrō iacēbat.
> *The slave, (**having been**) seriously **wounded**, was lying under the cart.*

3 In Stage 22 you met the *perfect active participle*:

> aegrōtī, deam **precātī**, remedium mīrābile spērābant.
> *The invalids, **having prayed to** the goddess, were hoping for a remarkable cure.*

4 Translate the following examples. Pick out the participle in each sentence and say whether it is present, perfect passive or perfect active:

  a ancillae, in vīllā labōrantēs, fūrem nōn vīdērunt.
  b servus, ā lībertō iussus, venēnum parāvit.
  c fēmina, marītum cōnspicāta, pecūniam celeriter cēlāvit.
  d mīlitēs urbem captam incendērunt.
  e Modestus captīvōs, ē carcere ēgressōs, invenīre nōn poterat.
  f Salvius in prīncipiīs stābat, saeviēns.

A participle is used to describe a noun. For example, in sentence **a** above, **labōrantēs** (*working*) describes **ancillae**. Find the nouns described by the participles in sentences **b–f**.

5 A participle agrees with the noun it describes in three ways: case, number and gender. For example:

nominative	**rēx**, in mediā turbā **sedēns**, dōna accipiēbat.
accusative	Quīntus **rēgem**, in mediā turbā **sedentem**, agnōvit.
singular	**lēgātus**, ad carcerem **regressus**, nēminem ibi invēnit.
plural	**custōdēs**, ad carcerem **regressī**, nēminem ibi invēnērunt.
masculine	**nūntius**, statim **profectus**, ad fundum contendit.
feminine	**uxor**, statim **profecta**, ad fundum contendit.

6 You have met the following forms of the participles:

a *Present participle*. For example: **trahēns** *dragging*.

	SINGULAR *masculine and feminine*	*neuter*	PLURAL *masculine and feminine*	*neuter*
nominative and vocative	trahēns	trahēns	trahentēs	trahentia
accusative	trahentem	trahēns	trahentēs	trahentia

Compare the endings of **trahēns** with the endings of the adjective **ingēns** on p. 148.

b *Perfect passive participle*. For example: **portātus** (*having been*) *carried*.

	SINGULAR *masculine*	*feminine*	*neuter*	PLURAL *masculine*	*feminine*	*neuter*
nominative and vocative	portātus (portāte)	portāta	portātum	portātī	portātae	portāta
accusative	portātum	portātam	portātum	portātōs	portātās	portāta

c *Perfect active participle*. For example: **ingressus** *having entered*.

	SINGULAR *masculine*	*feminine*	*neuter*	PLURAL *masculine*	*feminine*	*neuter*
nominative and vocative	ingressus (ingresse)	ingressa	ingressum	ingressī	ingressae	ingressa
accusative	ingressum	ingressam	ingressum	ingressōs	ingressās	ingressa

Compare the endings of **portātus** and **ingressus** with the endings of the adjective **bonus** on p. 148.

7 With the help of paragraph 6, find the Latin words for the participles in the following sentences:

a I saw the soldiers dragging the slave to prison.
b The girls, having been carried to safety, thanked their rescuers.
c The king, having entered, greeted the chieftains.

Uses of the subjunctive

The forms of the imperfect and pluperfect subjunctive are given on p. 157. The subjunctive can be used in several different ways, and its translation depends on the way it is being used in a particular sentence. In Book III you have met five uses of the subjunctive:

1   In Stage 24, you met the subjunctive used with **cum** (*when*):

> fabrī, cum pecūniam accēpissent, abiērunt.
> *When the workmen had received the money, they went away.*

Further examples:

a   Agricola, cum legiōnem īnspexisset, mīlitēs centuriōnēsque laudāvit.
b   cum haruspex in templō cēnāret, rēx ipse appropinquābat.

2   In Stage 25, you met the subjunctive used in *indirect questions*:

> cognōscere voluimus cūr multitūdō convēnisset.
> *We wanted to find out why the crowd had gathered.*
> (Compare this with the direct question:
> 'cūr multitūdō convēnit?' '*Why has the crowd gathered?*')

Notice a new meaning of **num** when used with an indirect question:

> equitēs fēminās rogāvērunt **num** fugitīvōs vīdissent.
> *The horsemen asked the women **whether** they had seen the fugitives.*
> (Compare this with the direct question:
> 'fugitīvōsne vīdistis?' '*Have you seen the fugitives?*')

Further examples:

a   incertus eram quam longum esset flūmen.
    (Compare: 'quam longum est flūmen?')
b   nēmō sciēbat num Modestus et Strȳthiō in Āfricā mīlitāvissent.
c   Rōmānī nesciēbant quot hostēs in castrīs manērent.
d   mē rogāvit num māter mea vīveret.

3   In Stage 26, you met the subjunctive used in *purpose clauses*:

> senātor mē arcessīvit ut rem hospitibus nārrārem.
> *The senator summoned me in order that I might tell my story to the guests.*
> Or, in more natural English:
> *The senator summoned me to tell my story to the guests.*

Further examples:

a   amīcī ad urbem festīnāvērunt ut auxilium cīvibus ferrent.
b   epistulam scrīpsī ut lēgātum dē perīculō monērem.

4 In Stage 27, you met the subjunctive used in *indirect commands*:

> dominus nōbīs imperāvit ut sellās lectōsque emerēmus.
> *The master ordered us to buy chairs and couches.*
> (Compare this with the direct command:
> 'sellās lectōsque emite!' *'Buy chairs and couches!'*)

Further examples:

a nūntius Britannīs persuāsit ut dōna ad aulam ferrent.
b senex deam Sūlem ōrāvit ut morbum sānāret.

5 In Stage 27, you also met the subjunctive used in *result clauses*:

> tanta erat stultitia iuvenum ut astrologō crēderent.
> *So great was the stupidity of the young men that they believed the astrologer.*

Further examples:

a tam dīligenter carcerem custōdīvī ut lēgātus ipse mē laudāret.
b mercātor tot statuās habēbat ut eās numerāre nōn posset.

6 To understand why a subjunctive is being used in a particular sentence, it is necessary to look at the whole sentence, and not just the subjunctive on its own. For example, study these two sentences; one contains a *result* clause, and the other contains a *purpose* clause:

a tam īrātus erat Agricola ut dormīre nōn posset.
Agricola was so angry that he could not sleep.
b Salvius mīlitēs ēmīsit ut Quīntum invenīrent.
Salvius sent out the soldiers to find Quintus.

Sentence **a** clearly contains the result clause: Agricola's failure to sleep was the *result* of his anger. The word **tam** (*so*) is a further clue; it is often followed by a result clause later in the sentence. Other similar words are **tantus** (*so great*), **tot** (*so many*) and **adeō** (*so* or *so much*).

Sentence **b** clearly contains the purpose clause: finding Quintus was the *purpose* of sending out the soldiers.

7 Translate the following examples:

a lībertus, cum venēnum bibisset, mortuus prōcubuit.
b tot hostēs castra nostra oppugnābant ut dē vītā dēspērārēmus.
c prīncipēs mē rogāvērunt cūr pontem trānsīre vellem.
d Gutta sub mēnsā sē cēlāvit ut perīculum vītāret.
e centuriōnēs mīlitibus imperāvērunt ut horrea reficerent.
f cum ancillae pōcula lavārent, quattuor equitēs ad tabernam advēnērunt.
g adeō attonitus erat fīlius meus ut diū immōtus stāret.
h iānuās cellārum aperuimus ut amīcōs nostrōs līberārēmus.
i amīcus mē monuit ut latērem.
j Modestus explicāre nōn poterat quō modō captīvī effūgissent.

In each sentence, find the reason why a subjunctive is being used.

Word order

The word order in the following sentences is very common:

1 In Book I, you met the following word order:

> dēspērābat senex.   *The old man was in despair.*

Further examples:

   a fūgit Modestus.
                 b revēnērunt mercātōrēs.

2 From Stage 21 onwards, you have met the following word order:

> dedit signum haruspex.   *The soothsayer gave the signal.*

Further examples:

   a rapuērunt pecūniam fūrēs.
        b īnspiciēbat mīlitēs Agricola.

3 From Stage 23 onwards, you have met the following word order:

> ēmīsit Salvius equitēs.   *Salvius sent out horsemen.*

Further examples:

   a tenēbat Cephalus pōculum.
        b posuērunt cīvēs statuam.

4 Further examples of all three types of word order:

   a discessit nūntius.
   b fēcērunt hostēs impetum.
   c reficiēbat mūrum faber.
   d poposcit captīvus aquam.
   e vexābant mē puerī.
   f periērunt īnfantēs.

5 Study the word order in the following phrases containing prepositions:

> in hāc prōvinciā
> *in this province*
>   ad nostrum patrem
>   *to our father*

From Stage 24 onwards, you have met a different word order:

> mediīs in undīs
> *in the middle of the waves*
>   hanc ad tabernam
>   *to this shop*

Further examples:

   a hāc in urbe
   b multīs cum mīlitibus
   c parvum ad oppidum
   d omnibus cum legiōnibus
   e tōtam per noctem
   f mediō in flūmine

Longer sentences

1 Study the following groups of sentences:

   a   puerī timēbant.
      The boys were afraid.

      puerī timēbant quod prope iānuam iacēbat ingēns canis.
      The boys were afraid because near the door was lying a huge dog.

      puerī timēbant quod prope iānuam iacēbat ingēns canis, vehementer lātrāns.
      The boys were afraid because near the door was lying a huge dog, barking loudly.

   b   Strȳthiōnem cōnspexit.
      He caught sight of Strythio.

      ubi ā culīnā redībat, Strȳthiōnem cōnspexit.
      When he was returning from the kitchen, he caught sight of Strythio.

      ubi ā culīnā in quā cēnāverat redībat, Strȳthiōnem cōnspexit.
      When he was returning from the kitchen in which he had been dining, he caught sight of Strythio.

   c   Salvius incertus erat.
      Salvius was uncertain.

      Salvius incertus erat quō fūgisset Dumnorix.
      Salvius was uncertain where Dumnorix had fled to.

      Salvius incertus erat quō fūgisset Dumnorix, cūr abesset Quīntus.
      Salvius was uncertain where Dumnorix had fled to, and why Quintus was missing.

2 Further examples:

   a   centuriō immōtus manēbat.
      centuriō immōtus manēbat, quamquam appropinquābant hostēs.
      centuriō immōtus manēbat, quamquam appropinquābant hostēs, quī hastās vibrābant.

   b   omnēs cīvēs plausērunt.
      ubi puellae cantāre coepērunt, omnēs cīvēs plausērunt.
      ubi puellae, quae prō pompā ambulābant, cantāre coepērunt, omnēs cīvēs plausērunt.

   c   nūntius prīncipia petīvit.
      nūntius quī epistulam ferēbat prīncipia petīvit.
      nūntius quī epistulam ferēbat, simulac ad castra advēnit, prīncipia petīvit.

3   Further examples of the longer types of sentences:

a   tantae erant flammae ut vīllam magnam dēlērent, quam architectus clārus aedificāverat.

b   lībertus cubiculum intrāre nōlēbat quod Memor, quī multum vīnum biberat, graviter iam dormiēbat.

c   Salvius, Belimicō diffīsus, tribūnum arcessīvit ut vērum cognōsceret.

d   postquam ad forum vēnimus, ubi mercātōrēs negōtium agere solēbant, rem mīrābilem vīdimus.

e   pater, cum fīliōs pōcula haurientēs cōnspexisset, vehementer saeviēbat.

f   Agricola mox cognōvit ubi hostēs castra posuissent, quot mīlitēs in castrīs essent, num equōs habērent.

Part Two: Vocabulary

Notes

1 Nouns and adjectives are listed as in the Book II Language Information section.

2 Verbs are usually listed in the following way:

the 1st person singular of the present tense, e.g. **pōnō** (*I place*);
the infinitive, e.g. **pōnere** (*to place*);
the 1st person singular of the perfect tense, e.g. **posuī** (*I placed*);
the perfect passive participle, e.g. **positus** (*having been placed*);
the meaning(s).

3 Study the following examples, listed in the way described in paragraph 2. Notice the typical ways in which the different conjugations form their perfect tense and perfect passive participle.

first conjugation
amō, amāre, amāvī, amātus   *love, like*
laudō, laudāre, laudāvī, laudātus   *praise*

second conjugation
moneō, monēre, monuī, monitus   *warn, advise*
terreō, terrēre, terruī, territus   *frighten*

third conjugation
Verbs of the third conjugation form their perfect tense and perfect passive participle in several different ways. Here are some of them:

dūcō, dūcere, dūxī, ductus   *lead*
neglegō, neglegere, neglēxī, neglēctus *neglect, ignore*
claudō, claudere, clausī, clausus   *shut, close*
mittō, mittere, mīsī, missus   *send*
fundō, fundere, fūdī, fūsus   *pour*
relinquō, relinquere, relīquī, relictus *leave*

fourth conjugation
custōdiō, custōdīre, custōdīvī, custōdītus *guard*
impediō, impedīre, impedīvī, impedītus   *hinder*

4 Use paragraph 3 to find the meaning of:

amāvī, laudātus, monitus, terrēre, ductus, neglēxī, clausus, mīsī, fundere, fūdī, relinquō, relictus, custōdītus, impedīvī.

5 Use the **Vocabulary** on pp. 170–84 to find the meaning of:

adiuvāre, comprehēnsus, nocēre, pāreō, patefēcī, prōditus, suscēpī, victus.

6 Some verbs have a perfect *active* participle, e.g. **locūtus** (*having spoken*). You have not yet met any other forms of these verbs and so this participle is the only form listed in the **Vocabulary**.

7 All words given in the **Vocabulary checklists** for Stages 1–28 are marked with an asterisk(*).

a

*ā, ab — *from; by*
*abeō, abīre, abiī — *go away*
absēns, *gen.* absentis — *absent*
*absum, abesse, āfuī — *be out, be absent, be away*
absurdus, absurda, absurdum — *absurd*
*ac — *and*
*accidō, accidere, accidī — *happen*
*accipiō, accipere, accēpī,
   acceptus — *accept, take in, receive*
accūsō, accūsāre, accūsāvī,
   accūsātus — *accuse*
*ad — *to, at*
addō, addere, addidī, additus — *add*
addūcō, addūcere, addūxī,
   adductus — *lead, lead on, encourage*
*adeō — *so much, so greatly*
*adeō, adīre, adiī — *approach, go up to*
*adeptus, adepta, adeptum — *having received, having
      obtained*
adest *see* adsum
adhibeō, adhibēre, adhibuī,
   adhibitus — *use*
adhūc — *up till now*
aditus, aditūs, m. — *opening*
*adiuvō, adiuvāre, adiūvī — *help*
administrō, administrāre,
   administrāvī, administrātus — *look after, manage*
adōrō, adōrāre, adōrāvī,
   adōrātus — *worship*
adstō, adstāre, adstitī — *stand by*
*adsum, adesse, adfuī — *be here, be present*
*adveniō, advenīre, advēnī — *arrive*
adventus, adventūs, m. — *arrival*
advesperāscit, advesperāscere,
   advesperāvit — *get dark, become dark*
*aedificium, aedificiī, n. — *building*
*aedificō, aedificāre, aedificāvī,
   aedificātus — *build*
*aeger, aegra, aegrum — *sick, ill*
aegrōtus, aegrōtī, m. — *invalid*
Aegyptius, Aegyptia,
   Aegyptium — *Egyptian*
Aegyptus, Aegyptī, f. — *Egypt*
afferō, afferre, attulī, adlātus — *bring*
afflīgō, afflīgere, afflīxī,
   afflīctus — *afflict, hurt*
ager, agrī, m. — *field*
*agitō, agitāre, agitāvī, agitātus — *chase, hunt*
*agmen, agminis, n. — *column (of men), procession*
agna, agnae, f. — *lamb*
*agnōscō, agnōscere, agnōvī,
   agnitus — *recognise*
*agō, agere, ēgī, āctus — *do, act*
   age! — *come on!*
   grātiās agere — *thank, give thanks*
   negōtium agere — *do business, work*
   persōnam agere — *play a part*
   vītam agere — *lead a life*
*agricola, agricolae, m. — *farmer*
ālea, āleae, f. — *dice*
*aliquis, aliquid — *someone, something*
   aliquid novī — *something new*
*alius, alia, aliud — *other, another, else*
   aliī … aliī — *some … others*
*alter, altera, alterum — *the other, the second*
altus, alta, altum — *deep*
amārus, amāra, amārum — *bitter*
ambō, ambae, ambō — *both*
*ambulō, ambulāre, ambulāvī — *walk*
amīcitia, amīcitiae, f. — *friendship*
*amīcus, amīcī, m. — *friend*
*āmittō, āmittere, āmīsī,
   āmissus — *lose*
*amō, amāre, amāvī, amātus — *love, like*
*amor, amōris, m. — *love*
amphitheātrum,
   amphitheātrī, n. — *amphitheatre*
amphora, amphorae, f. — *wine-jar*
amulētum, amulētī, n. — *amulet, lucky charm*
an — *or*
*ancilla, ancillae, f. — *slave-girl, maid*
angulus, angulī, m. — *corner*
angustus, angusta, angustum — *narrow*
*animus, animī, m. — *spirit, soul, mind*
   in animō volvere — *wonder, turn over in the
      mind*
*annus, annī, m. — *year*
*anteā — *before*
*ānulus, ānulī, m. — *ring*
anxius, anxia, anxium — *anxious*
*aperiō, aperīre, aperuī, apertus — *open*
apertē — *openly*
apodytērium, apodytēriī, n. — *changing-room*
*appāreō, appārēre, appāruī — *appear*
*appropinquō, appropinquāre,
   appropinquāvī — *approach, come near to*
aptus, apta, aptum — *suitable*
*apud — *among, at the house of*
*aqua, aquae, f. — *water*
Aquae Sūlis, Aquārum Sūlis,
   f.pl. — *Bath*
*āra, ārae, f. — *altar*
arānea, arāneae, f. — *spider, spider's web*
arca, arcae, f. — *strong-box, chest*
*arcessō, arcessere, arcessīvī,
   arcessītus — *summon, send for*
architectus, architectī, m. — *builder, architect*
*ardeō, ardēre, arsī — *burn, be on fire*
ārea, āreae, f. — *courtyard*
argenteus, argentea,
   argenteum — *made of silver*
arma, armōrum, n.pl. — *arms, weapons*
armārium, armāriī, n. — *chest, cupboard*
armō, armāre, armāvī,
   armātus — *arm*
armātī, armātōrum, m.pl. — *armed men*

arrogantia, arrogantiae, f. — *cheek, arrogance*
*ars, artis, f. — *art, skill*
ascendō, ascendere, ascendī — *climb, rise*
asinus, asinī, m. — *ass, donkey*
aspiciō, aspicere, aspexī — *look towards*
astrologus, astrologī, m. — *astrologer*
Athēnae, Athēnārum, f.pl. — *Athens*
*atque — *and*
ātrium, ātriī, n. — *atrium, main room, hall*
*attonitus, attonita, attonitum — *astonished*
*auctōritās, auctōritātis, f. — *authority*
auctus *see* augeō
audācia, audāciae, f. — *boldness, audacity*
audācter — *boldly*
*audāx, *gen.* audācis — *bold, daring*
*audeō, audēre — *dare*
*audiō, audīre, audīvī, audītus — *hear, listen to*
*auferō, auferre, abstulī, ablātus — *take away, steal*
augeō, augēre, auxī, auctus — *increase*
*aula, aulae, f. — *palace*
aureus, aurea, aureum — *made of gold, gold-plated*
aureus, aureī, m. — *gold coin*
auris, auris, f. — *ear*
*autem — *but*
*auxilium, auxiliī, n. — *help*
avāritia, avāritiae, f. — *greed*
avē atque valē — *hail and farewell*
avidē — *eagerly*

b

balneum, balneī, n. — *bath*
barba, barbae, f. — *beard*
barbarus, barbara, barbarum — *barbarian*
barbarus, barbarī, m. — *barbarian*
*bellum, bellī, n. — *war*
   *bellum gerere — *wage war, campaign*
*bene — *well*
beneficium, beneficiī, n. — *act of kindness, favour*
benignē — *kindly*
*benignus, benigna, benignum — *kind*
bēstia, bēstiae, f. — *wild beast*
*bibō, bibere, bibī — *drink*
blanditiae, blanditiārum, f.pl. — *flatteries*
blandus, blanda, blandum — *flattering*
*bonus, bona, bonum — *good*
*   melior, melius — *better*
   melius est — *it would be better*
*   optimus, optima, optimum — *very good, excellent, best*
bracchium, bracchiī, n. — *arm*
brevī — *in a short time*
brevis, breve — *short, brief*

Britannī, Britannōrum, m.pl. — *Britons*
Britannia, Britanniae, f. — *Britain*
Britannicus, Britannica, Britannicum — *British*

c

C. = Gāius
cachinnō, cachinnāre, cachinnāvī — *laugh, cackle, roar with laughter*
cadō, cadere, cecidī — *fall*
caecus, caeca, caecum — *blind*
*caelum, caelī, n. — *sky*
calceus, calceī, m. — *shoe*
Calēdonia, Calēdoniae, f. — *Scotland*
calliditās, calliditātis, f. — *cleverness, shrewdness*
*callidus, callida, callidum — *clever, cunning*
candidātus, candidātī, m. — *candidate*
*canis, canis, m. — *dog*
*cantō, cantāre, cantāvī — *sing, chant*
capillī, capillōrum, m.pl. — *hair*
*capiō, capere, cēpī, captus — *take, catch, capture*
   cōnsilium capere — *make a plan, have an idea*
captīvus, captīvī, m. — *prisoner, captive*
*caput, capitis, n. — *head*
*carcer, carceris, m. — *prison*
carnifex, carnificis, m. — *executioner*
*cārus, cāra, cārum — *dear*
casa, casae, f. — *small house*
*castra, castrōrum, n.pl. — *camp*
catēna, catēnae, f. — *chain*
caudex, caudicis, m. — *blockhead, idiot*
caupō, caupōnis, m. — *innkeeper*
causa, causae, f. — *reason, cause*
cautē — *cautiously*
cecidī *see* cadō
*cēdō, cēdere, cessī — *give in, give way*
celebrō, celebrāre, celebrāvī, celebrātus — *celebrate*
celer, celeris, celere — *quick, fast*
   celerrimus, celerrima, celerrimum — *very fast*
*celeriter — *quickly, fast*
   celerrimē — *very quickly, very fast*
   quam celerrimē — *as quickly as possible*
cella, cellae, f. — *cell, sanctuary*
*cēlō, cēlāre, cēlāvī, cēlātus — *hide*
*cēna, cēnae, f. — *dinner*
*cēnō, cēnāre, cēnāvī — *dine, have dinner*
*centum — *a hundred*
centuriō, centuriōnis, m. — *centurion*
cēpī *see* capiō
cēra, cērae, f. — *wax, wax tablet*
certāmen, certāminis, n. — *struggle, contest, fight*
certus, certa, certum — *certain, infallible*
   prō certō habēre — *know for certain*

cessī *see* cēdō

*cēterī, cēterae, cētera, pl. — *the others, the rest*

*cibus, cibī, m. — *food*

*circum — *around*

*circumspectō, circumspectāre, circumspectāvī — *look round*

circumveniō, circumvenīre, circumvēnī, circumventus — *surround*

*cīvis, cīvis, m.f. — *citizen*

clam — *secretly, in private*

*clāmō, clāmāre, clāmāvī — *shout*

*clāmor, clāmōris, m. — *shout, uproar*

*clārus, clāra, clārum — *famous, distinguished*

*claudō, claudere, clausī, clausus — *shut, close, block*

clēmēns, *gen.* clēmentis — *merciful*

Cn. = Gnaeus

*coepī — *I began*

*cōgitō, cōgitāre, cōgitāvī — *think, consider*

    sēcum cōgitāre — *consider to himself*

*cognōscō, cognōscere, cognōvī, cognitus — *get to know, find out*

*cōgō, cōgere, coēgī, coāctus — *force, compel*

cohors, cohortis, f. — *cohort*

colligō, colligere, collēgī, collēctus — *gather, collect, assemble*

colloquium, colloquiī, n. — *talk, chat*

colō, colere, coluī, cultus — *cultivate, make friends with*

columna, columnae, f. — *pillar, column*

*comes, comitis, m.f. — *comrade, companion*

cōmiter — *politely, courteously*

commemorō, commemorāre, commemorāvī — *talk about, mention, recall*

committō, committere, commīsī, commissus — *commit, begin*

*commodus, commoda, commodum — *convenient*

*commōtus, commōta, commōtum — *moved, alarmed, excited, distressed, upset*

*comparō, comparāre, comparāvī, comparātus — *obtain*

*compleō, complēre, complēvī, complētus — *fill*

*comprehendō, comprehendere, comprehendī, comprehēnsus — *arrest, seize*

*cōnficiō, cōnficere, cōnfēcī, cōnfectus — *finish*

*cōnfīdō, cōnfīdere — *trust*

coniūrō, coniūrāre, coniūrāvī — *plot, conspire*

cōnscendō, cōnscendere, cōnscendī — *climb on, embark on, go on board, mount*

*cōnsentiō, cōnsentīre, cōnsēnsī — *agree*

cōnsīdō, cōnsīdere, cōnsēdī — *sit down*

*cōnsilium, cōnsiliī, n. — *plan, idea, advice*

    cōnsilium capere — *make a plan, have an idea*

cōnsistō, cōnsistere, cōnstitī — *stand one's ground, stand firm, halt, stop*

cōnspectus, cōnspectūs, m. — *sight*

*cōnspicātus, cōnspicāta, cōnspicātum — *having caught sight of*

*cōnspiciō, cōnspicere, cōnspexī, cōnspectus — *catch sight of*

*cōnstituō, cōnstituere, cōnstituī, cōnstitūtus — *decide*

cōnsulō, cōnsulere, cōnsuluī, cōnsultus — *consult*

*cōnsūmō, cōnsūmere, cōnsūmpsī, cōnsūmptus — *eat*

contemnō, contemnere, contempsī, contemptus — *reject, despise*

*contendō, contendere, contendī — *hurry*

contentiō, contentiōnis, f. — *argument*

*contentus, contenta, contentum — *satisfied*

contineō, continēre, continuī — *contain*

continuus, continua, continuum — *continuous, on end*

contrārius, contrāria, contrārium — *opposite*

contumēlia, contumēliae, f. — *insult, abuse*

convalēscō, convalēscere, convaluī — *get better, recover*

*conveniō, convenīre, convēnī — *come together, gather, meet*

conversus, conversa, conversum — *having turned*

*coquō, coquere, coxī, coctus — *cook*

*coquus, coquī, m. — *cook*

*corpus, corporis, n. — *body*

corrumpō, corrumpere, corrūpī, corruptus — *corrupt*

*cotīdiē — *every day*

*crēdō, crēdere, crēdidī — *trust, believe, have faith in*

creō, creāre, creāvī, creātus — *make, create*

*crūdēlis, crūdēle — *cruel*

cruentus, cruenta, cruentum — *covered in blood*

*cubiculum, cubiculī, n. — *bedroom*

cucurrī *see* currō

cui (*dative of* quī) — *to whom, to which*

cuius (*genitive of* quī) — *whose, of which*

culīna, culīnae, f. — *kitchen*

*cum — (1) *when*

*cum — (2) *with*

*cupiō, cupere, cupīvī — *want*

*cūr? — *why?*

*cūra, cūrae, f. — *care*

*cūrō, cūrāre, cūrāvī — *look after, supervise*

*currō, currere, cucurrī — *run*

*custōdiō, custōdīre, custōdīvī, custōdītus — *guard*

*custōs, custōdis, m. — *guard*

d

damnō, damnāre, damnāvī, damnātus	condemn
dare *see* dō	
*dē	from, down from; about
*dea, deae, f.	goddess
*dēbeō, dēbēre, dēbuī, dēbitus	owe, ought, should, must
*decem	ten
dēcidō, dēcidere, dēcidī	fall down
decimus, decima, decimum	tenth
*dēcipiō, dēcipere, dēcēpī, dēceptus	deceive, fool
*decōrus, decōra, decōrum	right, proper
dedī *see* dō	
dēfendō, dēfendere, dēfendī, dēfēnsus	defend
dēfīxiō, dēfīxiōnis, f.	curse
dēiciō, dēicere, dēiēcī, dēiectus	throw down, throw
*deinde	then
*dēlectō, dēlectāre, dēlectāvī, dēlectātus	delight, please
*dēleō, dēlēre, dēlēvī, dēlētus	destroy
dēliciae, dēliciārum, f.pl.	darling
dēligō, dēligāre, dēligāvī, dēligātus	bind, tie, tie up
dēmittō, dēmittere, dēmīsī, dēmissus	let down, lower
*dēmōnstrō, dēmōnstrāre, dēmōnstrāvī, dēmōnstrātus	point out, show
dēmoveō, dēmovēre, dēmōvī, dēmōtus	dismiss
dēnārius, dēnāriī, m.	a denarius (coin)
*dēnique	at last, finally
dēnūntiō, dēnūntiāre, dēnūntiāvī, dēnūntiātus	denounce, reveal
dēpōnō, dēpōnere, dēposuī, dēpositus	put down, take off
dērīdeō, dērīdēre, dērīsī	mock, jeer at
dēscendō, dēscendere, dēscendī	come down
*dēserō, dēserere, dēseruī, dēsertus	desert
dēsiliō, dēsilīre, dēsiluī	jump down
dēsinō, dēsinere	end, cease
*dēspērō, dēspērāre, dēspērāvī	despair
dēstinō, dēstināre, dēstināvī, dēstinātus	intend
dēstringō, dēstringere, dēstrīnxī, dēstrictus	draw out, draw (a sword)
dētestātus, dētestāta, dētestātum	having cursed
*deus, deī, m.	god
dī immortālēs!	heavens above!

Dēva, Dēvae, f.	Chester
dēvorō, dēvorāre, dēvorāvī, dēvorātus	devour, eat up
*dīcō, dīcere, dīxī, dictus	say
dictō, dictāre, dictāvī, dictātus	dictate
*diēs, diēī, m.	day
diēs nātālis, diēī nātālis, m.	birthday
*difficilis, difficile	difficult
difficillimus, difficillima, difficillimum	very difficult
difficultās, difficultātis, f.	difficulty
diffīsus, diffīsa, diffīsum	having distrusted
*dignitās, dignitātis, f.	dignity, importance, prestige
dignus, digna, dignum	worthy, appropriate
*dīligenter	carefully, diligently
dīligentia, dīligentiae, f.	industry, hard work
dīligō, dīligere, dīlēxī, dīlēctus	be fond of
dīmittō, dīmittere, dīmīsī, dīmissus	send away, dismiss
dīrigō, dīrigere, dīrēxī, dīrēctus	steer
dīripiō, dīripere, dīripuī, dīreptus	pull apart, ransack
dīrus, dīra, dīrum	dreadful
dīs *see* deus	
*discēdō, discēdere, discessī	depart, leave
disciplīna, disciplīnae, f.	discipline, orderliness
*diū	for a long time
diūtius	any longer
dīxī *see* dīcō	
*dō, dare, dedī, datus	give
* poenās dare	pay the penalty, be punished
*doceō, docēre, docuī, doctus	teach
*doctus, docta, doctum	learned, educated, skilful, clever
*doleō, dolēre, doluī	hurt, be in pain
graviter dolēre	be extremely painful
dolus, dolī, m.	trickery
*domina, dominae, f.	mistress, madam
*dominus, dominī, m.	master
*domus, domūs, f.	home
domum redīre	return home
*dōnum, dōnī, n.	present, gift
*dormiō, dormīre, dormīvī	sleep
*dūcō, dūcere, dūxī, ductus	lead, take
*duo, duae, duo	two
*dūrus, dūra, dūrum	harsh, hard

e

*ē, ex	from, out of
ea	those things
eādem	the same

eam	her
eās	them
ēbrius, ēbria, ēbrium	drunk
*ecce!	see! look!
*efficiō, efficere, effēcī, effectus	carry out, accomplish
*effugiō, effugere, effūgī	escape
effundō, effundere, effūdī, effūsus	pour out
*ego, meī	I, me
mēcum	with me
*ēgressus, ēgressa, ēgressum	having gone out
*ēheu!	oh dear! oh no!
eī	to him, to her, to it
ēiciō, ēicere, ēiēcī, ēiectus	throw out
eīs	to them
eius	his, of him
ēlāpsus, ēlāpsa, ēlāpsum	having escaped
*ēligō, ēligere, ēlēgī, ēlēctus	choose
*ēmittō, ēmittere, ēmīsī, ēmissus	throw, send out
*emō, emere, ēmī, ēmptus	buy
ēn!	look!
ēn iūstitia!	so this is justice!
*enim	for
eō	from him
*eō, īre, iī	go
eōrum	their, of them
eōs	them
*epistula, epistulae, f.	letter
*eques, equitis, m.	horseman
equitō, equitāre, equitāvī	ride
*equus, equī, m.	horse
eram see sum	
ēripiō, ēripere, ēripuī, ēreptus	snatch, tear
errō, errāre, errāvī	make a mistake
longē errāre	make a big mistake
ērumpō, ērumpere, ērūpī, ēruptus	break away
est see sum	
ēsuriō, ēsurīre	be hungry
*et	and
et ... et	both ... and
*etiam	even, also
nōn sōlum ... sed etiam	not only ... but also
euge!	hurray!
*eum	him
*ex, ē	from, out of
exanimātus, exanimāta, exanimātum	unconscious
excipiō, excipere, excēpī, exceptus	receive
*excitō, excitāre, excitāvī, excitātus	arouse, wake up
*exclāmō, exclāmāre, exclāmāvī	exclaim, shout
excruciō, excruciāre, excruciāvī, excruciātus	torture, torment
*exeō, exīre, exiī	go out

exerceō, exercēre, exercuī, exercitus	practise, exercise
expellō, expellere, expulī, expulsus	throw out
*explicō, explicāre, explicāvī, explicātus	explain
explōrātor, explōrātōris, m.	scout, spy
exquīsītus, exquīsīta, exquīsītum	special
*exspectō, exspectāre, exspectāvī, exspectātus	wait for
extinguō, extinguere, exstīnxī, exstīnctus	extinguish, destroy
exstruō, exstruere, exstrūxī, exstrūctus	build
exsultō, exsultāre, exsultāvī	exult, be triumphant
extorqueō, extorquēre, extorsī, extortus	extort
*extrā	outside
extrahō, extrahere, extrāxī, extractus	pull out, take out
extulī see efferō	
exuō, exuere, exuī, exūtus	take off

---

f

*faber, fabrī, m.	craftsman, workman
*fābula, fābulae, f.	story, play
facēs see fax	
*facile	easily
*facilis, facile	easy
facinus, facinoris, n.	crime
*faciō, facere, fēcī, factus	make, do
impetum facere	charge, make an attack
sēditiōnem facere	revolt
fallō, fallere, fefellī, falsus	deceive
falsum, falsī, n.	lie, untruth
*falsus, falsa, falsum	false, untrue, dishonest
*faveō, favēre, fāvī	favour, support
fax, facis, f.	torch
fēcī see faciō	
fefellī see fallō	
fēlīx, gen. fēlīcis	lucky
*fēmina, fēminae, f.	woman
fenestra, fenestrae, f.	window
*ferō, ferre, tulī, lātus	bring, carry
graviter ferre	take badly
*ferōciter	fiercely
*ferōx, gen. ferōcis	fierce, ferocious
*fessus, fessa, fessum	tired
*festīnō, festīnāre, festīnāvī	hurry
fībula, fībulae, f.	brooch
*fidēlis, fidēle	faithful, loyal
*fidēs, fideī, f.	loyalty, trustworthiness
*fīlia, fīliae, f.	daughter
*fīlius, fīliī, m.	son
*flamma, flammae, f.	flame

* flōs, flōris, m. — flower
* flūmen, flūminis, n. — river
* fluō, fluere, flūxī — flow
* fōns, fontis, m. — fountain, spring
* fortasse — perhaps
* forte — by chance
* fortis, forte — brave
* fortiter — bravely
  fortūna, fortūnae, f. — fortune, luck
  fortūnātus, fortūnāta,
    fortūnātum — lucky
  forum, forī, n. — forum, market-place
  fossa, fossae, f. — ditch
* frāter, frātris, m. — brother
  fraus, fraudis, f. — trick
  frūmentum, frūmentī, n. — grain
* frūstrā — in vain
  fuga, fugae, f. — escape
* fugiō, fugere, fūgī — run away, flee (from)
  fugitīvus, fugitīvī, m. — fugitive
  fuī see sum
* fundō, fundere, fūdī, fūsus — pour
* fundus, fundī, m. — farm
  fūnus, fūneris, n. — funeral
* fūr, fūris, m. — thief
  furcifer, furciferī, m. — scoundrel
  furēns, gen. furentis — furious, in a rage
  fūstis, fūstis, m. — club, stick

g

  garriō, garrīre, garrīvī — chatter, gossip
  garum, garī, n. — sauce
* gaudeō, gaudēre — be pleased, rejoice
* gemitus, gemitūs, m. — groan
  gemma, gemmae, f. — gem, jewel
  gēns, gentis, f. — family, tribe
    ubi gentium? — where in the world?
  genū, genūs, n. — knee
* gerō, gerere, gessī, gestus — wear
*   bellum gerere — wage war, campaign
  gladiātor, gladiātōris, m. — gladiator
* gladius, gladiī, m. — sword
  Graecia, Graeciae, f. — Greece
  grātiae, grātiārum, f.pl. — thanks
*   grātiās agere — give thanks, thank
  grātīs — free
* gravis, grave — heavy, serious
* graviter — heavily, seriously, soundly
    graviter dolēre — be extremely painful
    graviter ferre — take badly
  gustō, gustāre, gustāvī — taste
  guttur, gutturis, n. — throat

h

* habeō, habēre, habuī, habitus — have
    in memoriā habēre — keep in mind, remember
    prō certō habēre — know for certain
    sermōnem habēre — have a conversation, talk
* habitō, habitāre, habitāvī — live
  hāc, hae, haec see hic
  haereō, haerēre, haesī — stick, cling
  haesitō, haesitāre, haesitāvī — hesitate
  hanc see hic
  haruspex, haruspicis, m. — soothsayer
  hās see hic
* hasta, hastae, f. — spear
  haud — not
  haudquāquam — not at all
  hauriō, haurīre, hausī,
    haustus — drain, drink up
  hercle! — by Hercules! good heavens!
  hērēs, hērēdis, m.f. — heir
* heri — yesterday
  heus! — hey!
* hic, haec, hoc — this
  hīc — here
  hiems, hiemis, f. — winter
  hilarē — in high spirits, merrily
  hinc — from here
  Hispānia, Hispāniae, f. — Spain
  hoc, hōc see hic
* hodiē — today
* homō, hominis, m. — human being, man
  homunculus, homunculī, m. — little man
* honor, honōris, m. — honour, public position
  honōrō, honōrāre, honōrāvī — honour
* hōra, hōrae, f. — hour
  horreum, horreī, n. — barn, granary
  hortātus, hortāta, hortātum — having encouraged
* hortus, hortī, m. — garden
  hōrum see hic
* hospes, hospitis, m. — guest, host
* hostis, hostis, m.f. — enemy
* hūc — here, to this place
  huic — to this (dative of hic)
  huius — of this (genitive of hic)
  humus, humī, f. — ground
*   humī — on the ground
  hunc see hic

i

* iaceō, iacēre, iacuī — lie
* iaciō, iacere, iēcī, iactus — throw
* iactō, iactāre, iactāvī, iactātus — throw
* iam — now
* iānua, iānuae, f. — door

ībam *see* **eō**		inimīcus, inimīcī, m.	*enemy*
*ibi	*there*	iniūria, iniūriae, f.	*injustice, injury*
id	*it*	innīxus, innīxa, innīxum	*having leant*
iecur, iecoris, n.	*liver*	innocēns, *gen.* innocentis	*innocent*
*igitur	*therefore, and so*	*inquit	*says, said*
*ignārus, ignāra, ignārum	*not knowing, unaware*	inquam	*I said*
*ignāvus, ignāva, ignāvum,	*lazy, cowardly*	īnsānia, īnsāniae, f.	*madness, insanity*
ignōtus, ignōta, ignōtum	*unknown*	īnsāniō, īnsānīre, īnsānīvī	*be mad, be insane*
iī *see* eō		īnsānus, īnsāna, īnsānum	*mad, crazy*
*ille, illa, illud	*that, he, she*	*īnsidiae, īnsidiārum, f.pl.	*trap, ambush*
illūc	*there, to that place*	īnsolēns, īnsolentis	*rude, insolent*
immineō, imminēre,		īnsolenter	*rudely, insolently*
imminuī	*hang over*	*īnspiciō, īnspicere, īnspexī,	
immortālis, immortāle	*immortal*	īnspectus	*look at, inspect, examine*
dī immortālēs!	*heavens above!*	*īnstruō, īnstruere, īnstrūxī,	
*immōtus, immōta, immōtum	*still, motionless*	īnstrūctus	*draw up*
*impediō, impedīre,		*īnsula, īnsulae, f.	*island*
impedīvī, impedītus	*delay, hinder*	īnsum, inesse, īnfuī	*be inside*
impellō, impellere, impulī,		*intellegō, intellegere,	
impulsus	*carry, push, force*	intellēxī, intellēctus	*understand*
*imperātor, imperātōris, m.	*emperor*	*intentē	*closely, carefully*
*imperium, imperiī, n.	*empire*	*inter	*among, between*
*imperō, imperāre, imperāvī	*order, command*	inter sē	*among themselves, with*
impetus, impetūs, m.	*attack*		*each other*
impetum facere	*charge, make an attack*	*intereā	*meanwhile*
impōnō, impōnere, imposuī,		*interficiō, interficere,	
impositus	*impose*	interfēcī, interfectus	*kill*
importō, importāre,		interrogō, interrogāre,	
importāvī, importātus	*import*	interrogāvī, interrogātus	*question*
imprecātiō, imprecātiōnis, f.	*curse*	*intrō, intrāre, intrāvī	*enter*
impulī *see* impellō		intulī *see* īnferō	
*in	*in, on; into, onto*	intus	*inside*
inānis, ināne	*empty, meaningless*	*inveniō, invenīre, invēnī,	
*incendō, incendere, incendī,		inventus	*find*
incēnsus	*burn, set on fire*	*invitō, invītāre, invītāvī,	
incēnsus, incēnsa, incēnsum	*inflamed, angered*	invītātus	*invite*
incertus, incerta, incertum	*uncertain*	*invītus, invīta, invītum	*unwilling, reluctant*
incidō, incidere, incidī	*fall*	iō!	*hurray!*
*incipiō, incipere, incēpī,		iocus, iocī, m,	*joke*
inceptus	*begin*	*ipse, ipsa, ipsum	*himself, herself, itself*
incitō, incitāre, incitāvī,		*īra, īrae, f.	*anger*
incitātus	*urge on, encourage*	*īrātus, īrāta, īrātum	*angry*
inclūsus, inclūsa, inclūsum	*shut up, imprisoned, trapped*	īre *see* eō	
incurrō, incurrere, incurrī	*run onto, collide, bump into*	irrumpō, irrumpere, irrūpī,	
indicium, indiciī, n.	*sign, evidence*	irruptus	*burst in, burst into*
induō, induere, induī,		*iste, ista, istud	*that*
indūtus	*put on*	*ita	*in this way*
inest *see* īnsum		* ita vērō	*yes*
īnfāns, īnfantis, m.	*child, baby*	ītalia, ītaliae, f.	*Italy*
*infēlīx, *gen.* īnfēlīcis	*unlucky*	*itaque	*and so*
*īnferō, īnferre, intulī,		*iter, itineris, n.	*journey, progress*
inlātus	*bring in, bring on*	*iterum	*again*
īnfestus, īnfesta, īnfestum	*hostile, dangerous*	*iubeō, iubēre, iussī, iussus	*order*
ingenium, ingeniī, n.	*character*	*iūdex, iūdicis, m.	*judge*
*ingēns, *gen.* ingentis	*huge*	iugulum, iugulī, n.	*throat*
ingravēscō, ingravēscere	*grow worse*	*iussum, iussī, n.	*instruction, order*
*ingressus, ingressa,		iūstitia, iūstitiae, f.	*justice*
ingressum	*having entered*	*iuvenis, iuvenis, m.	*young man*
iniciō, inicere, iniēcī,			
iniectus	*throw in*		
inimīcitia, inimīcitiae, f.	*feud, quarrel*		

l

L. = Lūcius
labefaciō, labefacere,
  labefēcī, labefactus — *weaken*
labor, labōris, m. — *work*
*labōrō, labōrāre, labōrāvī — *work*
labrum, labrī, n. — *lip*
*lacrima, lacrimae, f. — *tear*
*lacrimō, lacrimāre, lacrimāvī — *weep, cry*
laedō, laedere, laesī, laesus — *harm*
laetē — *happily*
*laetus, laeta, laetum — *happy*
lāpsus, lāpsa, lāpsum — *having fallen*
*lateō, latēre, latuī — *lie hidden*
lātrō, lātrāre, lātrāvī — *bark*
latrō, latrōnis, m. — *robber, thug*
*laudō, laudāre, laudāvī,
  laudātus — *praise*
lavō, lavāre, lāvī, lautus — *wash*
*lectus, lectī, m. — *couch, bed*
*lēgātus, lēgātī, m. — *commander*
*legiō, legiōnis, f. — *legion*
lēgō, lēgāre, lēgāvī, lēgātus — *bequeath*
*legō, legere, lēgī, lēctus — *read*
*lentē — *slowly*
*leō, leōnis, m. — *lion*
lēx, lēgis, f. — *law*
*libenter — *gladly*
*liber, librī, m. — *book*
*līberālis, līberāle — *generous*
līberī, līberōrum, m.pl. — *children*
*līberō, līberāre, līberāvī,
  līberātus — *free, set free*
*lībertus, lībertī, m. — *freedman, ex-slave*
lingua, linguae, f. — *tongue*
*lītus, lītoris, n. — *sea-shore, shore*
līvidus, līvida, līvidum — *lead-coloured*
*locus, locī, m. — *place*
*locūtus, locūta, locūtum — *having spoken*
longē — *far, a long way*
  longē errāre — *make a big mistake*
longus, longa, longum — *long*
loquāx, *gen.* loquācis — *talkative*
lucerna, lucernae, f. — *lamp*
lūdō, lūdere, lūsī — *play*
*lūna, lūnae, f. — *moon*

m

madidus, madida, madidum — *soaked through*
magicus, magica, magicum — *magic*
magnopere — *greatly*
*   maximē — *very greatly, very much, most of all*

*magnus, magna, magnum — *big, large, great*
  maior, *gen.* maiōris — *bigger, larger, greater*
*   maximus, maxima,
  maximum — *very big, very large, very great*
mālim — *I should prefer*
*malus, mala, malum — *evil, bad*
  peior, *gen.* peiōris — *worse*
*   pessimus, pessima,
  pessimum — *worst, very bad*
*mandātum, mandātī, n. — *instruction, order*
*mandō, mandāre, mandāvī,
  mandātus — *order, entrust, hand over*
*māne — *in the morning*
*maneō, manēre, mānsī — *remain, stay*
*manus, manūs, f. — *(1) hand*
*manus, manūs, f. — *(2) band (of men)*
*mare, maris, n. — *sea*
*marītus, marītī, m. — *husband*
Mārs, Mārtis, m. — *Mars (god of war)*
*māter, mātris, f. — *mother*
mātrimōnium, mātrimōniī,
  n. — *marriage*
*maximē — *very greatly, very much, most of all*

*maximus, maxima,
  maximum — *very big, very large, very great*
mē *see* ego
medicus, medicī, m. — *doctor*
*medius, media, medium — *middle*
*melior, melius — *better*
  melius est — *it would be better*
memoria, memoriae, f. — *memory*
  in memoriā habēre — *keep in mind, remember*
*mendāx, mendācis, m. — *liar*
mendāx, *gen.* mendācis — *lying, deceitful*
mēnsa, mēnsae, f. — *table*
mēnsis, mēnsis, m. — *month*
*mercātor, mercātōris, m. — *merchant*
meritus, merita, meritum — *well-deserved*
*metus, metūs, m. — *fear*
*meus, mea, meum — *my, mine*
  mī Quīnte — *my dear Quintus*
mihi *see* ego
*mīles, mīlitis, m. — *soldier*
mīlitō, mīlitāre, mīlitāvī — *be a soldier*
*mīlle — *a thousand*
*   mīlia — *thousands*
*minimē! — *no!*
*minimus, minima, minimum — *very little, least*
minor, *gen.* minōris — *less, smaller*
*mīrābilis, mīrābile — *extraordinary, strange*
misceō, miscēre, miscuī,
  mixtus — *mix*
*miser, misera, miserum — *miserable, wretched, sad*
  ō mē miserum! — *oh wretched me! oh dear!*
*mittō, mittere, mīsī, missus — *send*
*modus, modī, m. — *manner, way, kind*
*   quō modō? — *how? in what way?*
  rēs huius modī — *a thing of this kind*

molestus, molesta, molestum   *troublesome*

molliō, mollīre, mollīvī,
   mollītus   *soothe*

mollis, molle   *soft, gentle*

mōmentum, mōmentī, n.   *importance*

*moneō, monēre, monuī,
   monitus   *warn, advise*

*mōns, montis, m.   *mountain*

mora, morae, f.   *delay*

*morbus, morbī, m.   *illness*

(eī) moriendum est   *(he) must die*

*mors, mortis, f.   *death*

*mortuus, mortua, mortuum   *dead*

*mox   *soon*

multitūdō, multitūdinis, f.   *crowd*

multō   *much*

*multus, multa, multum   *much*

*   multī   *many*

*   plūs, *gen.* plūris   *more*

*   plūrimī, plūrimae, plūrima   *very many*

*   plūrimus, plūrima,
       plūrimum   *most*

*mūrus, mūrī, m.   *wall*

mūs, mūris, m.f.   *mouse*

—————— **n** ——————

*nam   *for*

*nārrō, nārrāre, nārrāvī,
   nārrātus   *tell, relate*

nāsus, nāsī, m.   *nose*

(diēs) nātālis, (diēī) nātālis,
   m.   *birthday*

*nauta, nautae, m.   *sailor*

*nāvigō, nāvigāre, nāvigāvī   *sail*

*nāvis, nāvis, f.   *ship*

*necesse   *necessary*

*necō, necāre, necāvī,
   necātus   *kill*

neglegēns, *gen.* neglegentis   *careless, taking no notice of*

neglegō, neglegere, neglēxī,
   neglēctus   *neglect, ignore, disregard*

*negōtium, negōtiī, n.   *business*

   negōtium agere   *do business, work*

*nēmō   *no one, nobody*

neque   *and not*

*   neque … neque   *neither … nor*

*nescio, nescīre, nescīvī   *not know*

niger, nigra, nigrum   *black*

*nihil   *nothing*

   nihil perīculī   *no danger*

nimis   *too*

*nimium   *too much*

nōbilis, nōbile   *noble, of noble birth*

nōbīs *see* nōs

*noceō, nocēre, nocuī   *hurt, harm*

noctū   *by night*

*nōlō, nōlle, nōluī   *not want*

   nōlī, nōlīte   *do not, don't*

*nōmen, nōminis, n.   *name*

*nōn   *not*

*nōnāgintā   *ninety*

*nōnne?   *surely?*

*nōnnūllī, nōnnūllae,
   nōnnūlla   *some, several*

nōnus, nōna, nōnum   *ninth*

*nōs   *we, us*

*noster, nostra, nostrum   *our*

*nōtus, nōta, nōtum   *known, well-known, famous*

*novem   *nine*

*nōvī   *I know*

*novus, nova, novum   *new*

*nox, noctis, f.   *night*

   noctū   *by night*

nūllus, nūlla, nūllum   *not any, no*

*num?   **(1)** *surely … not?*

*num   **(2)** *whether*

numerō, numerāre, numerāvī,
   numerātus   *count*

numerus, numerī, m.   *number*

*numquam   *never*

*nunc   *now*

*nūntiō, nūntiāre, nūntiāvī,
   nūntiātus   *announce*

*nūntius, nūntiī, m.   *messenger, news*

*nūper   *recently*

nusquam   *nowhere*

—————— **o** ——————

obdormiō, obdormīre,
   obdormīvī   *go to sleep*

obēsus, obēsa, obēsum   *fat*

obscūrus, obscūra,
   obscūrum   *dark, gloomy*

obstinātus, obstināta,
   obstinātum   *obstinate, stubborn*

*obstō, obstāre, obstitī   *obstruct, block the way*

obtulī *see* offerō

obviam eō, obviam īre,
   obviam iī   *meet, go to meet*

*occīdō, occīdere, occīdī,
   occīsus   *kill*

occupātus, occupāta,
   occupātum   *busy*

occupō, occupāre, occupāvī,
   occupātus   *seize, take over*

occurrō, occurrere, occurrī   *meet*

*octō   *eight*

*octōgintā   *eighty*

*oculus, oculī, m.   *eye*

ōdī   *I hate*

*offerō, offerre, obtulī,
   oblātus   *offer*

*ōlim	once, some time ago
ōmen, ōminis, n.	omen (sign from the gods)
omnīnō	completely
*omnis, omne	all
omnia	all, everything
*opēs, opum, f.pl.	money, wealth
*oppidum, oppidī, n.	town
opprimō, opprimere, oppressī, oppressus	crush
*oppugnō, oppugnāre, oppugnāvī, oppugnātus	attack
*optimē	very well
*optimus, optima, optimum	very good, excellent, best
optiō, optiōnis, m.	optio (military officer ranking below centurion)
ōrātiō, ōrātiōnis, f.	speech
ōrdō, ōrdinis, m.	row, line
ōrnāmentum, ōrnāmentī, n.	ornament, decoration
ōrnātus, ōrnāta, ōrnātum	decorated, elaborately furnished
*ōrnō, ōrnāre, ōrnāvī, ōrnātus	decorate
ōrō, ōrāre, ōrāvī	beg
ōs, ōris, n.	face
ōsculum, ōsculī, n.	kiss
*ostendō, ostendere, ostendī, ostentus	show

p

*paene	nearly, almost
pallēscō, pallēscere, palluī	grow pale
pallidus, pallida, pallidum	pale
pallium, palliī, n.	cloak
*parcō, parcere, pepercī	spare
parēns, parentis, m.f.	parent
*pāreō, pārēre, pāruī	obey
*parō, parāre, parāvī, parātus	prepare
*pars, partis, f.	part
*parvus, parva, parvum	small, little
minor, gen. minōris	less, smaller
* minimus, minima, minimum	very little, least
*passus, passa, passum	having suffered
pāstor, pāstōris, m.	shepherd
*patefaciō, patefacere, patefēcī, patefactus	reveal
*pater, patris, m.	father
patera, paterae, f.	bowl
patientia, patientiae, f.	patience
*paucī, paucae, pauca	few, a few
paulō	a little
*pāx, pācis, f.	peace
*pecūnia, pecūniae, f.	money
peior, gen. peiōris	worse
*per	through, along
perdomitus, perdomita, perdomitum	conquered

*pereō, perīre, periī	die, perish
perfidia, perfidiae, f.	treachery
perfidus, perfida, perfidum	treacherous, untrustworthy
perfuga, perfugae, m.	deserter
perīculōsus, perīculōsa, perīculōsum	dangerous
*perīculum, perīculī, n.	danger
periī see pereō	
perītē	skilfully
*perītus, perīta, perītum	skilful
permōtus, permōta, permōtum	alarmed, disturbed
perrumpō, perrumpere, perrūpī, perruptus	burst through, burst in
persecūtus, persecūta, persecūtum	having pursued
persōna, persōnae, f.	character
persōnam agere	play a part
*persuādeō, persuādēre, persuāsī	persuade
*perterritus, perterrita, perterritum	terrified
*perveniō, pervenīre, pervēnī	reach, arrive at
*pēs, pedis, m.	foot, paw
*pessimus, pessima, pessimum	worst, very bad
pestis, pestis, f.	pest, scoundrel
*petō, petere, petīvī, petītus	make for, attack; seek, beg for, ask for
*placeō, placēre, placuī	please, suit
*plaudō, plaudere, plausī, plausus	applaud, clap
plaustrum, plaustrī, n.	wagon, cart
*plēnus, plēna, plēnum	full
*plūrimus, plūrima, plūrimum	most, very much
* plūrimī, plūrimae, plūrima	very many
*plūs, gen. plūris	more
plūs vīnī	more wine
pōculum, pōculī, n.	wine-cup
*poena, poenae, f.	punishment
* poenās dare	pay the penalty, be punished
*poēta, poētae, m.	poet
poliō, polīre, polīvī, polītus	polish
pompa, pompae, f.	procession
*pōnō, pōnere, posuī, positus	place, put, put up
*pōns, pontis, m.	bridge
populus, populī, m.	people
porrō	what's more, furthermore
*porta, portae, f.	gate
*portō, portāre, portāvī, portātus	carry
*portus, portūs, m.	harbour
*poscō, poscere, poposcī	demand, ask for
*possum, posse, potuī	can, be able
*post	after, behind
*posteā	afterwards
*postquam	after, when

postrēmō	*finally, lastly*
*postrīdiē	*on the next day*
*postulō, postulāre, postulāvī, postulātus	*demand*
posuī *see* pōnō	
potēns, *gen.* potentis	*powerful*
potestās, potestātis, f.	*power*
potius	*rather*
potuī *see* possum	
*praebeō, praebēre, praebuī, praebitus	*offer, provide*
*praeceps, *gen.* praecipitis	*headlong*
praeficiō, praeficere, praefēcī, praefectus	*put in charge*
*praemium, praemiī, n.	*prize, reward, profit*
praesertim	*especially*
praestō, praestāre, praestitī	*show, display*
praetereā	*besides*
prāvus, prāva, prāvum	*evil*
*precātus, precāta, precātum	*having prayed (to)*
precēs, precum, f.pl.	*prayers*
prēnsō, prēnsāre, prēnsāvī, prēnsātus	*take hold of, clutch*
pretiōsus, pretiōsa, pretiōsum	*expensive, precious*
*pretium, pretiī, n.	*price*
prīmum	*first*
*prīmus, prīma, prīmum	*first*
in prīmīs	*in particular*
*prīnceps, prīncipis, m.	*chief, chieftain*
prīncipia, prīncipiōrum, n.pl.	*headquarters*
prius	*earlier*
*prō	*in front of, for, in return for*
prō certō habēre	*know for certain*
probus, proba, probum	*honest*
*prōcēdō, prōcēdere, prōcessī	*advance, proceed*
prōcumbō, prōcumbere, prōcubuī	*fall down*
prōcūrātor, prōcūrātōris, m.	*manager*
prōdō, prōdere, prōdidī, prōditus	*betray*
profectus, profecta, profectum	*having set out*
prōgressus, prōgressa, prōgressum	*having advanced*
prohibeō, prohibēre, prohibuī, prohibitus	*prevent*
*prōmittō, prōmittere, prōmīsī, prōmissus	*promise*
prōmoveō, prōmovēre, prōmōvī, prōmōtus	*promote*
*prope	*near*
prōpōnō, prōpōnere, prōposuī, prōpositus	*propose, put forward*
prōspiciō, prōspicere, prōspexī	*look out*
prōvincia, prōvinciae, f.	*province*
*proximus, proxima, proximum	*nearest*
prūdēns, *gen.* prūdentis	*shrewd, intelligent, sensible*

prūdentia, prūdentiae, f.	*shrewdness, intelligence, good sense*
psittacus, psittacī, m.	*parrot*
*puella, puellae, f.	*girl*
*puer, puerī, m.	*boy*
pugiō, pugiōnis, m.	*dagger*
*pugna, pugnae, f.	*fight*
*pugnō, pugnāre, pugnāvī	*fight*
*pulcher, pulchra, pulchrum	*beautiful*
*pulsō, pulsāre, pulsāvī, pulsātus	*hit, knock at, punch*
*pūniō, pūnīre, pūnīvī, pūnītus	*punish*
pūrgō, pūrgāre, pūrgāvī, pūrgātus	*clean*

q

quā *see* quī	
*quadrāgintā	*forty*
quae *see* quī	
*quaerō, quaerere, quaesīvī, quaesītus	*search for, look for*
*quālis, quāle	*what sort of*
*quam	*(1) how*
quam celerrimē	*as quickly as possible*
*quam	*(2) than*
quam	*(3) see* quī
*quamquam	*although*
*quantus, quanta, quantum	*how big*
quārtus, quārta, quārtum	*fourth*
*quattuor	*four*
*-que	*and*
*quī, quae, quod	*who, which*
*quicquam (*also spelt* quidquam)	*anything*
quid?	*what?*
quid vīs?	*what do you want?*
quīdam	*one, a certain*
quidem	*indeed*
quiētus, quiēta, quiētum	*quiet*
quīngentī, quīngentae, quīngenta	*five hundred*
*quīnquāgintā	*fifty*
*quīnque	*five*
quīntus, quīnta, quīntum	*fifth*
*quis? quid?	*who? what?*
*quō?	*(1) where? where to?*
quō	*(2) see* quī
*quō modō?	*how? in what way?*
*quod	*(1) because*
quod	*(2) see* quī
*quondam	*one day, once*
*quoque	*also, too*
quōs *see* quī	
*quot?	*how many?*
quotiēns	*whenever*

r

rapiō, rapere, rapuī, raptus — *seize, grab*
raptim — *hastily, quickly*
raucus, rauca, raucum — *harsh*
*recipiō, recipere, recēpī, receptus — *recover, take back*
recitō, recitāre, recitāvī, recitātus — *recite*
recumbō, recumbere, recubuī — *lie down, recline*
*recūsō, recūsāre, recūsāvī, recūsātus — *refuse*
*reddō, reddere, reddidī, redditus — *give back, make*
*redeō, redīre, rediī — *return, go back, come back*
reditus, reditūs, m. — *return*
redūcō, redūcere, redūxī, reductus — *lead back*
*referō, referre, rettulī, relātus — *bring back, carry, deliver, tell, report*
reficiō, reficere, refēcī, refectus — *repair*
*rēgnum, rēgnī, n. — *kingdom*
*regressus, regressa, regressum — *having returned*
*relinquō, relinquere, relīquī, relictus — *leave*
remedium, remediī, n. — *cure*
repetō, repetere, repetīvī, repetītus — *claim*
rēpō, rēpere, rēpsī — *crawl*
*rēs, rēī, f. — *thing*
   rem cōgitāre — *consider the problem*
   rem cōnficere — *finish the job*
   rem intellegere — *understand the truth*
   rem nārrāre — *tell the story*
   rem suscipere — *undertake the task*
   rēs contrāria — *the opposite*
*resistō, resistere, restitī — *resist*
*respondeō, respondēre, respondī — *reply*
retineō, retinēre, retinuī, retentus — *keep, hold back*
rettulī *see* referō
*reveniō, revenīre, revēnī — *come back, return*
*rēx, rēgis, m. — *king*
*rīdeō, rīdēre, rīsī — *laugh, smile*
rīdiculus, rīdicula, rīdiculum — *ridiculous, silly*
rīpa, rīpae, f. — *river bank*
*rogō, rogāre, rogāvī, rogātus — *ask*
Rōmānī, Rōmānōrum, m.pl. — *Romans*
Rōmānus, Rōmāna, Rōmānum — *Roman*
*ruō, ruere, ruī — *rush*
*rūrsus — *again*

s

*sacer, sacra, sacrum — *sacred*
*sacerdōs, sacerdōtis, m.f. — *priest*
sacrificium, sacrificiī, n. — *offering, sacrifice*
sacrificō, sacrificāre, sacrificāvī, sacrificātus — *sacrifice*
*saepe — *often*
saeviō, saevīre, saeviī — *be in a rage*
*saevus, saeva, saevum — *savage, cruel*
saltātrīx, saltātrīcis, f. — *dancing-girl*
saltō, saltāre, saltāvī — *dance*
*salūtō, salūtāre, salūtāvī, salūtātus — *greet*
*salvē! — *hello!*
sānē — *obviously*
*sanguis, sanguinis, m. — *blood*
sānō, sānāre, sānāvī, sānātus — *heal, cure*
sānus, sāna, sānum — *well, healthy*
*sapiēns, *gen.* sapientis — *wise*
sapientia, sapientiae, f. — *wisdom*
*satis — *enough*
saxum, saxī, n. — *rock*
scaena, scaenae, f. — *stage, scene*
*scelestus, scelesta, scelestum — *wicked*
scelus, sceleris, n. — *crime*
*scio, scīre, scīvī — *know*
scrība, scrībae, m. — *scribe, secretary*
*scrībō, scrībere, scrīpsī, scrīptus — *write*
*sē — *himself, herself, themselves*
   inter sē — *among themselves, with each other*
   sēcum — *with him, with her, with themselves*
   sēcum cōgitāre — *consider to himself*
sēcrētus, sēcrēta, sēcrētum — *secret*
secundus, secunda, secundum — *second*
secūtus, secūta, secūtum — *having followed*
*sed — *but*
*sedeō, sedēre, sēdī — *sit*
sēditiō, sēditiōnis, f. — *rebellion*
   sēditiōnem facere — *revolt*
sella, sellae, f. — *chair*
sēmirutus, sēmiruta, sēmirutum — *half-collapsed, rickety*
*semper — *always*
*senātor, senātōris, m. — *senator*
*senex, senis, m, — *old man*
*sententia, sententiae, f. — *opinion*
*sentiō, sentīre, sēnsī, sēnsus — *feel, notice*
sepeliō, sepelīre, sepelīvī, sepultus — *bury*
*septem — *seven*
septimus, septima, septimum — *seventh*
*septuāgintā — *seventy*

sermō, sermōnis, m. — conversation
    sermōnem habēre — have a conversation, talk
*servō, servāre, servāvī, servātus — save, look after, preserve
*servus, servī, m. — slave
*sex — six
*sexāgintā — sixty
*sī — if
  sibi *see* sē
*sīc — thus, in this way
  siccō, siccāre, siccāvī, siccātus — dry
*sīcut — like
  significō, significāre, significāvī, significātus — mean, indicate
  signō, signāre, signāvī, signātus — sign, seal
*signum, signī, n. — sign, seal, signal
  silentium, silentiī, n. — silence
*silva, silvae, f. — wood
*simulac, simulatque — as soon as
  sine — without
  situs, sita, situm — situated
  sōlācium, sōlāciī, n. — comfort
*soleō, solēre — be accustomed
  sollemniter — solemnly
*sollicitus, sollicita, sollicitum — worried, anxious
  sōlum — only
    nōn sōlum … sed etiam — not only … but also
*sōlus, sōla, sōlum — alone, lonely, only, on one's own
  solūtus, solūta, solūtum — relaxed
  sonitus, sonitūs, m. — sound
  sordidus, sordida, sordidum — dirty
  soror, sorōris, f. — sister
*spectāculum, spectāculī, n. — show, spectacle
  spectātor, spectātōris, m. — spectator
*spectō, spectāre, spectāvī, spectātus — look at, watch
  spernō, spernere, sprēvī, sprētus — despise, reject
  spērō, spērāre, spērāvī — hope, expect
*spēs, speī, f. — hope
  splendidus, splendida, splendidum — splendid
  squālidus, squālida, squālidum — covered in dirt, filthy
*statim — at once
  statiō, statiōnis, f. — post
  statua, statuae, f. — statue
  stilus, stilī, m. — pen, stick
*stō, stāre, stetī — stand
  stola, stolae, f. — dress
  strēnuē — hard, energetically
  strepitus, strepitūs, m. — noise, din
  studium, studiī, n. — enthusiasm, keenness
  stultitia, stultitiae, f. — stupidity
*stultus, stulta, stultum — stupid
*suāvis, suāve — sweet

*sub — under, beneath
*subitō — suddenly
  subveniō, subvenīre, subvēnī — help, come to help
*sum, esse, fuī — be
*summus, summa, summum — highest, greatest, top
  sūmptuōsē — lavishly
  sūmptuōsus, sūmptuōsa, sūmptuōsum — expensive, lavish
*superō, superāre, superāvī, superātus — overcome, overpower
*surgō, surgere, surrēxī — get up, rise
  suscipiō, suscipere, suscēpī, susceptus — undertake, take on
*suspicātus, suspicāta, suspicātum — having suspected
  suspīrium, suspīriī, n. — heart-throb
  sustulī *see* tollō
  susurrō, susurrāre, susurrāvī — whisper, mutter
*suus, sua, suum — his, her, their, their own
    suī, suōrum, m.pl. — his men

————— t —————

  T. = Titus
*taberna, tabernae, f. — shop, inn
  tabernārius, tabernāriī, m. — shopkeeper
  tablīnum, tablīnī, n. — study
  tabula, tabulae, f. — tablet, writing tablet
*taceō, tacēre, tacuī — be silent, be quiet
    tacē! — shut up! be quiet!
*tacitē — quietly, silently
*tacitus, tacita, tacitum — quiet, silent, in silence
*tālis, tāle — such
*tam — so
*tamen — however
  tamquam — as, like
*tandem — at last
  tantum — only
*tantus, tanta, tantum — so great, such a great
  tardus, tarda, tardum — late
  tē *see* tū
  tēctum, tēctī, n. — ceiling, roof
*templum, templī, n. — temple
*temptō, temptāre, temptāvī, temptātus — try
  tenebrae, tenebrārum, f.pl. — darkness
*teneō, tenēre, tenuī, tentus — hold
  tergum, tergī, n. — back
*terra, terrae, f. — ground, land
*terreō, terrēre, terruī, territus — frighten
  terribilis, terribile — terrible
  tertius, tertia, tertium — third
  testāmentum, testāmentī, n. — will
*testis, testis, m.f. — witness
  thermae, thermārum, f.pl. — baths
  tibi *see* tū

*timeō, timēre, timuī — be afraid, fear
tintinō, tintināre, tintināvī — ring
toga, togae, f. — toga
*tollō, tollere, sustulī, sublātus — raise, lift up, hold up
tormentum, tormentī, n. — torture
torqueō, torquēre, torsī, tortus — torture
*tot — so many
*tōtus, tōta, tōtum — whole
*trādō, trādere, trādidī, trāditus — hand over
*trahō, trahere, trāxī, tractus — drag
trāns — across
*trānseō, trānsīre, trānsiī — cross
tremō, tremere, tremuī — tremble, shake
*trēs, tria — three
tribūnal, tribūnālis, n. — platform
tribūnus, tribūnī, m. — tribune (high-ranking officer)
triclīnium, triclīniī, n. — dining-room
*trīgintā — thirty
tripodes, tripodum, m.pl. — tripods
*trīstis, trīste — sad
*tū, tuī — you (singular)
  tēcum — with you (singular)
tulī see ferō
*tum — then
tunica, tunicae, f. — tunic
*turba, turbae, f. — crowd
*tūtus, tūta, tūtum — safe
*tuus, tua, tuum — your, yours (singular)

u

*ubi — where, when
ubīque — everywhere
ūllus, ūlla, ūllum — any
*ultimus, ultima, ultimum — furthest
ultiō, ultiōnis, f. — revenge
ululō, ululāre, ululāvī — howl
umerus, umerī, m. — shoulder
*umquam — ever
*unda, undae, f. — wave
*unde — from where
*ūnus, ūna, ūnum — one
*urbs, urbis, f. — city
ursa, ursae, f. — bear
*ut — (1) as
*ut — (2) that, so that, in order that
utrum ... an — whether ... or
*uxor, uxōris, f. — wife

v

vah! — ugh!
*valdē — very much, very
*valē — goodbye, farewell
varius, varia, varium — different
*vehementer — violently, loudly
velim, vellem see volō
vēnātiō, vēnātiōnis, f. — hunt
*vēndō, vēndere, vēndidī, vēnditus — sell
venēnātus, venēnāta, venēnātum — poisoned
*venēnum, venēnī, n. — poison
venia, veniae, f. — mercy
*veniō, venīre, vēnī — come
venter, ventris, m. — stomach
*ventus, ventī, m. — wind
vēr, vēris, n. — spring
*verberō, verberāre, verberāvī, verberātus — strike, beat
*verbum, verbī, n. — word
versus, versa, versum — having turned
*vertō, vertere, vertī, versus — turn
  sē vertere — turn round
*vērum, vērī, n. — truth, the truth
vērus, vēra, vērum — true, real
vester, vestra, vestrum — your (plural)
vestīmenta, vestīmentōrum, n.pl. — clothes
*vexō, vexāre, vexāvī, vexātus — annoy
*via, viae, f. — street
vibrō, vibrāre, vibrāvī, vibrātus — wave, brandish
vīcī see vincō
victī, victōrum, m.pl. — the conquered
victima, victimae, f. — victim
victor, victōris, m. — victor, winner
victōria, victōriae, f. — victory
vīcus, vīcī, m. — town, village
*videō, vidēre, vīdī, vīsus — see
*vīgintī — twenty
vīlla, vīllae, f. — house, villa
vinciō, vincīre, vīnxī, vīnctus — bind, tie up
*vincō, vincere, vīcī, victus — conquer, win, be victorious
  victī, victōrum, m.pl. — the conquered
*vīnum, vīnī, n. — wine
*vir, virī, m. — man
*virtūs, virtūtis, f. — courage
vīs, f. — force, violence
vīs see volō
vīsitō, vīsitāre, vīsitāvī, vīsitātus — visit
*vīta, vītae, f. — life
*vītō, vītāre, vītāvī, vītātus — avoid
*vituperō, vituperāre, vituperāvī, vituperātus — blame, curse

*vīvō, vīvere, vīxī — live, be alive
vīvus, vīva, vīvum — alive, living
*vix — hardly, scarcely, with difficulty

vōbīs *see* vōs
*vocō, vocāre, vocāvī, vocātus — call
*volō, velle, voluī — want
    quid vīs? — what do you want?
    velim — I should like

volvō, volvere, volvī, volūtus — turn
    in animō volvere — wonder, turn over in the mind
*vōs — you (plural)
*vōx, vōcis, f. — voice
*vulnerō, vulnerāre, vulnerāvī, vulnerātus — wound, injure
*vulnus, vulneris, n. — wound
vult *see* volō